Sounds Like an Ending

Midnight Oil, 10-1 and Red Sails in the Sunset

Glen Humphries

Last Day of School
lastdayofschool.net

ISBN: 978-0648032359

Sounds Like an Ending is copyright Glen Humphries 2018

For more information or to tell me how fantastic this book was email dragstermag@hotmail.com. If you loved it so much that you want to buy some more copies then head over to my micropublishing site Last Day of School (www.lastdayofschool.net)

This book is copyright. All rights reserved. Except for private study, research, criticism or reviews, as permitted under the Copyright Act, no part of this book may be reproduced, stored in a retrieval system, or transmitted in any form or by any means without prior written permission. So be nice and don't rip things off from this book and pretend you wrote it yourself. That would be much appreciated. Incidentally, as I'm a guy with a close-cropped haircut, I've long wondered how Peter Garrett maintains his clean-shaven dome. It's hard to shave your own head – either with clippers or a razor – as it's so easy to miss bits. I assume his wife helps him out at home, but when the band is touring who takes care of it? Does he do it himself every day? Or is it the daily job of one of the roadies to climb on a stepladder with a razor and shaving foam and get to work?

A catalogue record of this book is available from the National Library of Australia.

About the author

Glen Humphries is a journalist with a hobby of writing and self-publishing books via his micro-publishing arm Last Day of School. He started with his first book *The Slab: 24 Stories of Beer in Australia* (which was the national winner in the worldwide Gourmand food and drink writing awards) and then just kept going. Since then he has published two other books about beer, as well as a biography of First Fleet convict James Squire and a collection of stories about bands in his hometown of Wollongong. That last one includes a number of stories about those local longhairs by the name of Tumbleweed. He has interviewed Peter Garrett once and Rob Hirst several times and only got a little bit starstruck. To him, Jim Moginie has often seemed like the odd guy out in the band, the guy who stood still onstage surrounded by four other guys playing the band equivalent of a demolition derby. The footage in the *Midnight Oil: 1984* doco where the band comes offstage and has cups of tea still cracks him up. Before *Red Sails in the Sunset*, he'd never heard of a guy called Jimmy Sharman. He believes the album should be referred to as *10-1* in conversation, not *10, 9, 8* and certainly not *10,9,8,7,6,5,4,3,2,1*. He thinks it's a quirk of geography; Australians say *10-1* while the rest of the world says *10, 9, 8*. The Australians are correct. He has never liked the song *Beds Are Burning*, and is pretty sure that will make him unpopular with Midnight Oil fans. His favourite Midnight Oil album is *Red Sails in the Sunset*. As you're soon to find out.

Also by Glen Humphries and published by Last Day of School

The Slab: 24 Stories of Beer in Australia
James Squire: The Biography
The Six-Pack: Stories from the World of Beer
Friday Night at the Oxford
Beer Is Fun!

Aboriginal and Torres Strait Islanders are advised that this book contains the names of people who have passed away.

Track listing

1 Foreword by Jeff Apter

7 Introduction

11 Before …

21 10,9,8,7,6,5,4,3,2,1

Side One

33 Outside World

38 Only the Strong

43 Short Memory

52 Read About It

60 Scream in Blue

Side Two

66 US Forces

72 Power & the Passion

82 Maralinga

94 Tin-Legs & Tin Mines

100 Somebody's Trying to Tell Me Something

107 Red Sails in the Sunset

Side One

119 When the Generals Talk
126 Best of Both Worlds
134 Sleep
140 Minutes to Midnight
151 Jimmy Sharman's Boxers
160 Bakerman

Side Two

167 Who Can Stand in the Way
173 Koscuisko
180 Helps Me Helps You
191 Harrisburg
198 Bells and Horns in the Back of Beyond
203 Shipyards of New Zealand

209 Acknowledgements
211 Bibliography

Foreword
by Jeff Apter

I'll never forget the first time I saw Midnight Oil. It was April 1978, so I was – what? – 16. A typical spotty suburban teenager. Bad hair. Not much of an idea about the world beyond my western suburbs/housing commission bubble. Frequently stoned. The total catastrophe. But I did love music.

Every Tuesday night my friends and I had a ritual. We would take the lengthy commute from Padstow station all the way to St James in the city, counting off each of the dozen or so stops. Once in town, our first port of call was the statue of Captain Cook in Hyde Park; when viewed from just the right angle, it appeared that Cookie was grasping something other than a telescope in his hand. That was always good for a snicker. Then it was on to the New Zealand Hotel at the bottom end of William St. OK, not actually into the New Zealand Hotel; instead we'd loiter outside, hoping the tallest and stubbliest of our group would be served some beers, which he'd then stealthily deliver to us.

The next stage of our journey was traversing the flotsam and jetsam of William St, the hookers and trannies and junkies that would loiter near the steps leading to our final destination. These were not the type of night people I met in Padstow. (I don't think Padstow actually had night people, come to think of it.) Interestingly, I can't ever recall being propositioned: I guess the working girls (and boys) figured, with some justification, that we were not exactly swimming in cash.

Then, finally, we reached Double J's Studio 221, which was located just off the red-light heart of Darlinghurst. I usually felt mixed emotions as I stood outside with my friends, waiting to get in. I'd be excited to find out who was playing, but I also felt way outside of my natural habitat: 221 was the domain of the cool crowd, the inner-city Double J set, uni students, for Christ's sake. We suburban shitkickers were interlopers, no doubt about it.

Anyway, on this particular night, we hustled inside and snagged a good spot, right at the front of where the band was set up (there was no actual stage; they played at floor level). I recall a bottle being passed around; maybe even a spliff. As we sat there, I noticed this odd-looking character seated directly in front of me. He was tall – *no, he was fucking huge* – and a straw hat covered his hefty dome, which was an odd touch, this being a time when hats typically came in two varieties: terry and towelling. Another freak, I figured, but then the lights went down, his hat came off – and Peter Garrett came to life before my very eyes.

I was completely freaked out by this chrome-domed rock and roll gargantuan; he flung himself about like he'd been zapped by a cattle prod. It wasn't really dancing – it was as though the music was flowing right through him. And when he sang – and I'd never heard the Oils before – I got the feeling that he meant every single word.

This was intense (and keep in mind this was a time when that word actually meant something) and really exciting. A bit scary, too. The band was amazing, striking all the right poses. The pencil-thin Martin Rotsey had the 'smouldering ciggie in the neck of your guitar' move down pat. Rob Hirst played like his drum stool was on fire. Jim Moginie was all business, likewise Andrew James on bass. It was hugely impressive. You didn't see bands like this in the front bar of the Padstow Park Hotel.

I was hooked; we all were. From Studio 221 it was on to any number of apocalyptic Oils gig – I remember a Balmain Town Hall gig a few weeks later and the Before the Bomb Hall at the Paddington Town Hall in November 1978. Afterwards, in the bowels of Town Hall station, I bumped into a guy from school ('You're an Oils fan?' I couldn't believe it) who was banging out an Oils song on a tin drum – the sound boomed around Platform 22, reminding me of that ominous line in their song *Dust* about the inherent dangers to be found at "2am in Town Hall station". There was also the night at Sydney's Stagedoor Tavern, a short stumble from Central Station, where Garrett kept whacking his melon against the low-hanging pipes and ended the gig covered in blood. That show was called "Death to Disco"; I duly went out and had a T-shirt made that read: "Disco Shit".

Plenty happened to Midnight Oil between my first encounters and their landmark album, *10...1*, so brilliantly brought to life here by Glen Humphries. They morphed from the chosen act of the Double J set to a band of the people, filling hefty venues all around the place – I even saw them play at Blacktown – Blacktown! – and setting their gaze on the rest of the world.

And these songs are great; they'd moved on from the likes of *Surfing with a Spoon* and *Run by Night*, which drew me to them in the first place, to the way more powerful and important (a term I use warily when talking rock and roll) *US Forces*, *Only the Strong*, *Power and the Passion* and the rest of them. It's not often a studio album tracklist reads like a best-of.

OK, I'm never going to be a spotty teenager again, and thank goodness for that. But with this terrific insight into a peerless album, Glen Humphries has helped me relive a hugely influential musical experience from my past. I'm so inspired, in fact, that I'm tempted to check out ole' Captain Cook again, and see if he's still manhandling that telescope …

6 | SOUNDS LIKE AN ENDING

Introduction

You know that feeling when someone puts down something you really, really like? That combination of shock and outrage, followed by a burning desire to prove to that person just how wrong they are, how the thing you like is truly, truly awesome?

Well, that's where this book started. From a desire to defend *Red Sails in the Sunset* from those who were inclined to put it in the "Psst, this album's a bit shit" pile.

Because those people are so misguided. *Red Sails in the Sunset* isn't shit. Not even a little bit. While a lot of albums can feel dated due to being very much a product and a reflection of their time both sonically and in their subject matter, *Red Sails* still stands up today. It's the sound of a band very much in their own bubble and doing what feels right for them, rather than trying to reflect what else is going on in the world of music. It still sounds weird, sometimes strange and gloriously different; unlike anything else that was released in the mid-1980s. The album has a sense of timelessness some of their other releases lack – it really could have been recorded at any time in the 30-odd years.

And yet there is hate for this marvellous release. Those in and outside the band view it as a mis-step in their career. How an album that gave the band its first No1 can be viewed like that is a mystery to me.

The authors of *The 100 Best Australian Albums* claim "the experimentation overpowered the songs". In his book on the band, Michael Lawrence says it's "an orgy of studio trickery" and gives album track *Bakerman* the only one-star grade out of the band's entire recorded catalogue.

Even the band's main songwriters seems to have little love for it. Rob Hirst said "it wasn't nearly as focused as its predecessor", while Jim Moginie says the *Red Sails* album sounds like a band short on good songs – "... we didn't really have the goods". Though he also acknowledges some people really like it so he wouldn't put it down.

The band itself put *Red Sails in the Sunset* down with their next release. The four-track EP *Species Deceases* was designed to be the opposite of *Red Sails*; instead of spending an age in the studio, they went in and laid the tracks down in a few days. Even the short and sharp nature of an EP seems to be a backhander directed at the "studio trickery" of *Red Sails*.

And so I was inspired to do something to stand up for the *Sails*. I threw *10-1* in here as well, partly because these two albums are how I discovered the band and are still how I see the band today. The two releases are an undeniable pair – the band at its most expressive and experimental. Additionally, *10-1* provides you with a road map to show how the band got to the place to make and release *Red Sails*.

Finally, a few words on the title of the book. Fans have no doubt recognised it as a line from *Red Sails* tune *Minutes to Midnight*. In terms of these two albums, it's an especially apt name because, as you will see, in the recording of both albums there was the very real potential that either one of them could have broken the band for different reasons. Each could have been the last thing we ever heard from Midnight Oil.

10 | SOUNDS LIKE AN ENDING

Before ...

They could have been called Schwampy Moose. And I feel pretty secure in saying that nobody now thinks that was a good idea. That was the name of the band in the early 1970s when it was Rob Hirst on drums and vocals, Andrew "Bear" James on bass and some shy awkward kid named Jim Moginie on guitar. There were two other guys – one of whom played flute. Yeah, a flute. So rock and roll.

Some might like to think that, if they heard the very early recordings of their favourite band, they could hear signs of what was to come. That's not possible with Schwampy Moose. In a brave decision, the band included a Schwampy Moose track in their Overflow Tank collection. And you'd have to assume they picked the best of those tracks available to them. It's Hirst shouting "Schwampy Moose!" over a bassline from Bear while Moginie comes in with a fumbling guitar riff. It all ends with a bashed-out drum solo from Hirst that calls to mind a drumkit being kicked down a flight of stairs.

Fortunately they would improve. And, in 1971, they changed their name to Sparta, which was a much better name. Then, via a November 1973 ad for a singer in the *Sydney Morning Herald* of all places, they find a very big piece of the puzzle. A tall long-haired blonde guy by the name of Peter Garrett knocked on the door and got the gig. There may have been other people audition but no one in the band remembers any of them – the shock of seeing this towering dude must have wiped any other singers from the memory banks (though journalist David Leser said he also auditioned for the job behind the microphone).

They gave Garrett the gig – partially because of his striking appearance and partially because he had his own PA. He would also bring with him a love of the band Skyhooks, which Moginie would credit with redirecting their songwriting. "Pete introduced us to Skyhooks, who we thought were just a pop band because they wore funny clothes," he told Radio National's Robbie Buck. "What they were on about was a very Australian subject matter and it was a very post-Whitlam era when we came up, so that obviously rubbed off in us in terms of lyric writing."

But Garrett would take a while to fully commit to the band as he was working through his law studies in Canberra. A year later he joined Farm full-time – for they had changed their name again. Showing an impressive amount of drive for a young band, they set up a tour of venues on the NSW South Coast, touting themselves as "top Sydney rock band Farm" (ahh, the things you could get away with in the days before the internet).

Around the same time another piece of the puzzle joined in the form of cool guitarist Martin Rotsey – though various biographies don't make it clear whether he joins before or after Garrett becomes the full-time singer. Sometime after those two guys had joined, out came the hat of keyboardist Peter Watson (who would himself soon be excess to requirements). In the hat would go suggestions for a new band name. Yes, they were changing it again.

The names that went in vary depending on who is telling the story. In his autobiography Garrett said he scrawled Southern Cross and Television on scraps of paper and chucked them in. He also said Hirst put the dreaded Schwampy Moose in the hat, along with Sparta. But it was the poor keyboard player Watson who wrote down the name of the band he would soon end up leaving – Midnight Oil. Hirst's reason for

Watson getting punted would be because he alienated the band by unbuttoning his shirt to expose his chest onstage "and would shake his mane as he played Rick Wakeman-esque keyboards". Though perhaps someone who wanted to name the band Schwampy Moose shouldn't throw too many stones.

By 1978 the band started building its supporter base around Sydney with the only people in the music industry paying attention being the-then Double J and magazines like *RAM*. That magazine would run an early story by journalist Andrew McMillan would name the band as Rob Hurst, Martin Rossi, Jim Migini, K Sprint (James) and Peter Garrett. Not to worry, in about five years Australia would know their names.

In 1978 they released their debut album – which would be fondly referred to as "the Blue Meanie" by fans – on their own Powderworks label. Oddly, the album was distributed by Seven Records, the music arm of the Seven Network – one of the commercial networks unlikely to give the band much airtime. Still, without a lot of radio or TV attention, this debut from an independent band reached No43 on the charts. Needless to say it surprised many in Australian music circles who thought the band had little going for it.

A year later, their second album would blow the doors off their debut. Called *Head Injuries* (after the original title of the song that would later become *I Don't Wanna be the One*), it was produced by Les Karski. Hirst would remember Karski's mission as getting the band to strip out all the wanky "hippie waffle" of their debut. And he did, with the album more closely resembling the urgency of their live shows. The songs are good enough to overlook the fact there are only nine of them there. It contained the live firecracker of *Stand in Line*, with a James-created bassline that would make his replacements Peter Gifford and Bones Hillman work hard to play (though, to be fair, Giffo does play on the definitive version recorded live at Parramatta Park in 1982 and released as the B-side of *Armistice Day* and later would form part of the *Overflow Tank* collection).

The album went to the top of the alternative charts and reached gold status by 1980. That year, James' health problems led to him leaving the band. His replacement was Canberra carpenter Peter Gifford, who got a real baptism of fire via the infamous Stagedoor Tavern gig. The band was booked to play the last night before the Sydney venue near Central station was to close down. The venue had promoted the gig, saying the band were going to "destroy the Stagedoor" that night. And the police believed it; they interviewed Garrett before the show, sought an injunction to stop the gig, cordoned off a few blocks around the venue and had the riot squad out and about.

"The whole thing was lit up with spotlights," Gifford told the band's biographer Dodshon. "The police were out in significant numbers – hundreds. I remember they wouldn't open the back door, it was positively dangerous."

With nearly 1000 punters in a room meant to hold just 300, no air conditioning and the police refusing to allow the fire doors to be opened, the band considered cancelling but figured that would cause its own problems. They played the show, left the stage drenched in sweat and some of them deathly pale from the lack of fresh air. The oxygen tank the band kept backstage at all their gigs was well used that night.

On July 22nd and 23rd, Gifford got the chance to record with the band for the first time. At the helm was *Head Injuries* producer Les Karski and the resulting *Bird Noises* EP really sounds like a companion to that album, as evidenced by the first words heard on the EP – Garrett's "let's rock" demand.

It's an EP that also contained the first real sign of the band's willingness to try something unexpected. I'm of course talking about that instrumental with the beautiful title of *Wedding Cake Island*. It was written by

Rotsey and Moginie, reportedly in the former's Coogee flat while looking out the window at the island in question (there are two explanations put forward for the name – the island looks like a wedding cake when the whitewater breaks over it giving the illusion of "icing" or loads of bird crap on the island make it look like icing on a cake).

A lovely surf instrumental, it was the band's first real chart success – breaking into the top 10 singles chart at No9 a month after the EP's November 1980 release. It surely confused a lot of people who would hear this instrumental tune and then go to the record store to pick up the EP. There they would be confronted by the rather nightmarish cover image of a baby bird crying out, or perhaps reaching to its mother for food. "Surely this couldn't be the record that contained that lovely song," they must have thought to themselves.

Surprisingly, the song would do time as an encore. After the sweaty roar of an Oils show, it was *Wedding Cake Island* that allowed the audience – and the band – to catch their breath before the headlong rush to the end of the show created in the last two songs of the encore.

A year later, the band headed to the UK to record with esteemed producer Glyn Johns. While his Rolling

Stones-The Who heyday was well and truly past him, having Johns behind the desk surely seemed like a coup for the band. It was a chance to record the album that would hopefully enable the band to move up a few rungs on the rock and roll ladder.

It didn't turn out that way. Rather that recording in London as they'd expected, the band found themselves in a new studio on Johns' country farm. The producer would rush off to London at regular intervals, leaving the band at a loose end. Gifford used that time to put his carpenter skills to use, building a few cupboards in the kitchen, a house for the farm's ducks and repairing one of Johns' wooden trailers.

A fractious relationship with Johns in the studio made the recording less than enjoyable. A sense of homesickness made the resulting album very Australian in flavour, with references to Ned Kelly, the Tasmanian town of Burnie, quinellas and the lucky country. Sonically, the album sounds flat and a little lifeless, especially when compared to the urgency of the band's two previous efforts. Even the album opener *Don't Wanna Be The One* lacks punch. That song – indeed the whole album – sounds muffled, as though someone has put a cardboard box in front of the speakers.

All of this might be why the band's label A&M

decided to pass on the album (though not before trying unsuccessfully to get the band to go back into the studio to record "a hit"). So the band returned to Australia with the *Place Without a Postcard* recordings, which would end up reaching No12 on the album charts. They toured Australia to pay back the overdraft at the Chatswood branch of the ANZ Bank and wondered what they were going to do next.

The band surely could not have foreseen that what they'd end up doing next would change everything. And for the better too.

20 | SOUNDS LIKE AN ENDING

10, 9, 8, 7, 6, 5, 4, 3, 2, 1

Released November 1982

22 | SOUNDS LIKE AN ENDING

Okay, so am I the only one who sees it as a little curious that a band who made a thing out of not appearing on ABC TV music show *Countdown* actually named one of their seminal albums after a countdown?

It's an album title that counts down from 10 to one, just like the climax of every episode of the long-running TV show. It's more likely the album title came from the concept of the countdown to a missile launch, as with *10-1* we enter the pair of albums more focused than others on the idea of nuclear warfare (though it's an idea that would dominate *Red Sails in the Sunset* more).

Still one does wonder if the album title was a sly dig at the show. The subject does rate a few mentions over the end credits of *Only The Strong*, a DVD covering the making of the album. Hirst mentioned the title referred to a "countdown to war". Then it cuts to Jim Moginie who made a reference to the TV show and said the title was Garrett's idea. Cut to Garrett, who said, "I think it was more the nuclear issue at the time, but of course it had a bit of a spoof quality to it because of the *Countdown* show. But I actually can't remember." I'll take a punt and suggest there's a little bit more than coincidence at play here.

It may not be the first time they had a whack at *Countdown* through their music – some suggest the "middle-aged queens" line in *Stand in Line* is a reference to the show's host Ian "Molly" Meldrum.

Being the band who never played on *Countdown* is a key part of the band's legend. In an episode of MusicMax's *The Artist's Story*, Moginie reckoned not appearing on the show properly worked better for the band than if they had. "Not going on *Countdown* was the thing we probably benefitted from, even though it came from our hearts," Moginie said. "We really detested the whole *Countdown* thing, presenting bands in a naff way."

Peter Garrett seemed to think so little of the 'not appearing on *Countdown*' thing that he didn't mention it at all in his autobiography. He did speak about it with Helen Thomas for her 1986 book about the Australian music scene, *Pay to Play*. There, he said they *were* going to appear on the show. It was the idea of their manager Gary Morris, as long as the band could design their own set to fit in with their already well-defined image.

Garrett said the show agreed to that request but, when the day came they said no. "We came to Melbourne to liaise with them on set and we were presented with the book of rules about what you can and can't do, where the cameras would be, where the flashing lights would be, and we said 'Look, sorry, it's just not going to happen'. We blew it out."

There's a different take on this in Molly Meldrum's biography, *The Never, Um, Ending Story*. The story there goes that *Countdown* producer Ted Emery was told by the higher-ups to crack down on bands being late to filming sessions. The next band to be late after that edict came down? Midnight Oil. They had played a show in Sydney the night before and flew down early in the morning.

Meldrum also said the band wanted to do their own lights and sound, which was never going to happen in a unionised shop like the ABC. "So I have a feeling that when the Oils' management was refused permission to take charge of the sound and lighting, they were purposely late for rehearsal, knowing what the end result would be."

Original bassist Andrew James offers another take in his online autobiography. James said *Countdown* had already prepared a blue set for the band to perform *Run By Night*. They arrived in Melbourne on the morning of the shoot – Saturday, April 7 – after a late gig the night before and went to the hotel to catch up on some sleep, while Morris headed to the studio.

When he got there he discovered the *Countdown* team was expecting the band to be there at 8am, rather than being asleep in a St Kilda hotel. "Gary was a cocky young buck who thought he could talk anyone round," James wrote. "Words followed between Gary and the *Countdown* staff, with the result that another band was enlisted to appear on the show in the place of Midnight Oil that day."

Given James' date of April 7 for the recording that means the Oils were due to appear on the episode airing on April 8, 1979. Checking out the "live" bands on that episode we can see which ones likely got their chance at the expense of Midnight Oil. The options are guitar and piano duo Moscos & Stone or a band called Atlantis with their first single *Winner*. Neither of those names rings any bells with me (though they can be seen on YouTube) so it's safe to say Midnight Oil didn't make way for a band of the future.

Whichever side of the fence the truth lies, it seems there's one thing both sides agree on. That is, Midnight Oil *were* going to appear on *Countdown*. Despite all the subsequent protestations about the show being "naff", the band had arranged a filming session in the

Countdown studio and even booked flights to Melbourne to appear in front of the cameras. As Rob Hirst said of *Countdown* in that episode of *The Artist's Story*, "We nearly did it." In his autobiography James said the idea the band refused to play on the show "wasn't quite true, but it made good press".

Perhaps in the early 1980s they may have given a brief thought to popping their heads into the *Countdown* studio, as they were looking for a bit of a leg-up career-wise. In June 1981 the band had headed to England to record what would be their third album *Place Without a Postcard*. At the helm was Glyn Johns, who had worked with the likes of The Who, Led Zeppelin, The Rolling Stones and The Beatles.

This was going to be the band's big break, the album that would pull them out of the pub circuit in the capital cities and into bigger venues, the album that would catch the ears of music fans in the suburbs of Australia and start the next phase of their career.

But it didn't. According to biographer Mark Dodshon, several members of the band hated the experience of recording with Johns. And it seems the producer didn't think much of those months in mid-1981 either; he only mentions Midnight Oil once in his autobiography *Sound Man* – as part of a list of artists who recorded in his farmhouse studio.

The band's international record label A&M didn't think much of the album, delivering the standard record company complaint – "we can't hear any hits. Go back and record some" (a weird complaint for an album that opens with perennial fan favourite *Don't Wanna Be The One*). Not at all surprisingly, the band refused and so the label threw tapes at the band and effectively said "don't let the door hit your arses on the way out".

The band had travelled halfway around the world to write what was a very Australian album. So when they signed a deal with a new record company to release *Place Without a Postcard*, it went well in the band's home – reaching No12 on the charts. But it really didn't do much business anywhere else. So the album the band had hoped would take them to the next level ended up leaving them in the same place. That place included being heavily in debt to the Chatswood branch of the ANZ bank and having to tour relentlessly around the country to get out of the red. So maybe, just for a moment they thought, "hey, an appearance on *Countdown* might get us out of this hole".

Instead, they did something that seems a bit insane; they put themselves in debt again and went back to England in September 1982 to record the next album. "We took the gamble of going back to London and living in pretty bad conditions," Hirst said in *Your Name's on the Door,* "not knowing whether we were going to spend the rest of our lives paying off this record that we'd decided to embark upon."

Once over there, they connected with this young producer called Nick Launay, who had a brief CV that included the messy noise of The Birthday Party's *Release the Bats*. Go and listen to that song and it becomes clear the band made a risky decision to pick Nick. Perhaps even more so when he started coming up with what to the band were weird ideas – overdubbing, multi-tracking, recording the drums without any cymbals, cutting various takes of songs to pieces and then reassembling the finished product with an intro from one song, a verse from another, a guitar solo from here and a middle eight from there.

It certainly added to the truckloads of pressure the band was feeling at the time. The way some members saw it, this album they were recording with this Launay kid was the band's last chance. It could end up being the swansong of Midnight Oil. In a wide-ranging interview with Depth Perception podcast Moginie said the second time they went to London was "make or break".

"This was at the point where we were really at the end of our tether," he said. "We thought whatever we do now is going to be make or break. We had a lot of soul-searching going on around that album."

Hirst, who was having panic attacks during the recording of *10-1*, repeated the "make or break" line in both his book *Willie's Bar and Grill* and on a special on the band's videos for MusicMAX. In that TV interview, he told host Chit Chat that the band was at breaking point from the stress of the moment.

"There was a lot of frustration in the band," Hirst said.

"Arguments were breaking out with the band. I remember Jim saying, 'I don't think I can stand this much longer. I'm out'. There was tension between Nick Launay and Gary, our manager, in the studio".

Hirst himself said he had a nervous breakdown due to being unhappy about the fact the band was burning through money while staying in England and the pressure of needing this album to be a success.

Infighting. Money worries. Nervous breakdowns. Career pressures. If you were a gambler, you'd lay down money that this new album would stiff; with maybe a side bet on the band breaking up before its release.

And yet, most likely because of what Hirst categorised as the band's "desperate bloody-mindedness" the album *10,9,8,7,6,5,4,3,2,1* did alright. Okay, well it did better than alright. When it was released in November 1982 it ended up going platinum seven times over, peaked at No3 on the album charts and was still in the top 100 two years later when the follow-up *Red Sails in the Sunset* was released.

Moginie, the musical mad scientist in the band, was pretty chuffed with what they'd come up with. He told the Depth Perception podcast *10-1* was "a real joy" to make.

"That was the first record I ever made that I came out of just feeling really proud of it," Moginie said.

"It was one of those albums where you feel like your dream's come true and you can't believe you've done it."

For Garrett it was a case of a whole lot of things aligning at the same time.

"It just came at a good time in the band's career," he told Noise11.com's Edina Patsy in 2016. "We were angry, we were young, we were hungry. But we were focused and I think that Rob Hirst's writing in particular came to the fore. And Jim's as well but the writing really started to come together. We also caught Nick Launay at a really good time in his career where he was really willing to go out on a ledge and see what he could do. A combination of those circumstances gave us that recording."

But as for it going platinum? Well that was a surprise to Garrett, he admitted in the book *Pay to Play* in 1986. "The fact that it went to triple platinum or whatever totally flabbergasted, surprised, stunned and amazed us."

The album's success probably made Mr Willis, the manager of the ANZ branch at Chatswood, very happy too. Legend has it he'd been approving the band's increasingly large overdraft without seeking approval from the head office.

Side One

Outside World
(Moginie)
4.24

So there they are in a recording studio in Shepherd's Bush in London; a producer whom one of the band members described as a "hyperactive stick insect" and a tall, gangly man with a bald head. They've stayed back to mix this new album they've made while the rest of the band has flown home to Australia.

And the first song hasn't even finished and the tall bald one has found something to laugh about. "Wait until the kids in Mullimbimby hear this," he says of the album. The stick insect producer has no idea what he's on about so he explains how that song, and so much else on this new album, is going to be really unexpected by the fans. Those fans – who are mostly male – are used to blaring out the Oils rock anthems through the speakers of panel van stereos after a surf at the beach or getting a bit of aggro out in the sweaty front rows at one of the band's live shows. This first song, he says, will do their heads in.

That's how journalist Barry Divola saw it in a *10-1* retrospective for *Rolling Stone* in 2012. And he's really got a point. The last thing the band had left the fans was *Lucky Country*, the closing track from the *Place Without a Postcard* album. That started with a deep bassline groove before the reliable jagged guitar riffs of the Oils come in the verses. Sure, there sounds like there might be a little bit of keyboard in there but it's right at the back of the mix. But the way the song closes out with the chant of the song title, that's the Oils, man. And it's a song that goes off live.

So November 1982 finds these fans preparing for an Australian summer, getting around in tight fluoro boardshorts and tank tops that seem all the rage in those days. Just in time for summer, the Oils have released their new album and across the continent people slide a tape of *10,9,8,7,6,5,4,3,2,1* into the stereo of their panel van or drop it on the turntable in their room. Their expectations raised, they press play or drop the needle on the start of the first song.

And the first thing they hear? A keyboard and what sounds like some electronic synthesiser, then maybe even some violins. "What the hell is this?" they ask themselves. Maybe they think the guy at the record store put the wrong album in the cover, so they walk over to the record player and rotate their head around as they try and read the spinning label. Nope, it says this is a Midnight Oil record.

Wait, that sounds like Garrett's voice, they think. But is he trying to sing like a pop star. And the guitars, they wonder, where are they? If this is supposed to be Midnight Oil, there are supposed to be guitars. Oh, wait, there's a guitar – four minutes into this strange, strange song. But even then, it sounds like they've put some odd effect on it.

The fans scratch their heads and think, this really wasn't what they were expecting.

For that they can blame Jim Moginie. That weird-sounding *Outside World* was all his idea. It's the only song on the album credited to one songwriter and only the third solo songwriting credit from any Midnight Oil album to date. Incidentally, all three of these are Moginie efforts; the others being *Nothing Lost – Nothing Gained* (the longest song the band ever recorded) from the first album and *I'm the Cure* from the *Bird Noises* EP.

Moginie decided it was time to be a bit weird for this make or break album. And it makes sense in a perverse way; the straight-out rock attack the band had made their stock in trade up to this point didn't seem to be enough to push them to the next level. So maybe weirdness was the way to go.

He told the Depth Perception podcast that the realisation about breaking out of the rock genre came from a residency in London's ZigZag Club ahead of the recording sessions. They played loud and it sounded like crap and so they bought smaller amps and, lo and behold, the gig sounded better.

That led Moginie to think they could get rid of "all the external faff, all the noise and distortion".

"It slowly started to dawn on us that we didn't have to do the normal thing," he said. "Certain members of the band weren't keen. Some got a bit fearful about this change in direction."

Placing *Outside World* as the opening track was really a case of the band nailing their colours to the mast. They could have opted for one of the songs that sounded more like the Oils everyone knew – like, say, *Read About It* – to open the innings. You know, ease people into the change. But no, they went for the weird with *Outside World.*

"*Outside World* was certainly not a Midnight Oil song in the true sense of the word," Moginie told Depth Perception, "but that was what was in the air with the band at the time. That kind of song could get through because it had a good lyric, it had a good foundation."

Though he also admitted it was "going to completely fuck them up" when it was released in Australia.

As for what the song is about, well, over-reading the meaning of songs can be fun, so let's try it. That last album *Place Without a Postcard*, found the band in England and looking back home – at least in terms of the songs. There they were on the other side of the world and ended up writing what would be very Australian songs.

So maybe what we have here in *Outside World* is a tacit admission that they've decided to start looking at places other than Australia for things to write about.

Or maybe the lyrics are only of secondary importance to the music. Maybe the main intent of the song is, as they say, to completely fuck people up.

Only The Strong
(Hirst/Moginie)
4.31

All those Midnight Oil fans who were left scratching their heads at the weirdness of the opening track no doubt felt a bit better about 26 seconds into track two. After wading through 25 seconds that had them thinking, "jeez, they must have forgotten to hit the stop button after they finished recording the first song" (but which sneakily has a bit from both songs, acting as a neat segue from one to the next) they get the bald one screaming about being locked in his room.

Any thought to what that might mean is cast to the wind when the guitars and drums come in, seemingly fighting each other to be the first musical notes we hear. The guitars and drums tumble and jostle for position until they take a breather for that line about eating and sleeping. Then in comes the song's signature sound, that guitar tremolo riff that is so good it gets space on the track all to itself.

If they haven't already, the fans reach for the volume knob and crank it way up when those drums and guitars again race in. After about two verses where Hirst plays the snare but almost no kick drum (which is weird from a drummer's point of view) he turns the middle of the tune into an aggressive drumming clinic as though his kit did something to piss him off.

On top of all the sound and fury sits Garrett's vocals. He chooses to almost whisper the first few lines, as though he's confessing something to us. Then his voice takes on a tone of angst and desperation. And when he sings of wanting to scream, it really is done with a scream. There's an urgency in the way Garrett sings the song's title. Sometimes it's accompanied by grunts or panting breaths, as though it's giving him a sense of release.

There's such a frantic nature to the song that the acoustic-guitar driven minute-long outro comes as a relief, giving the listener a chance to catch a few breaths.

Jesus, the fans listening in their panel vans in November 1982 think, why the hell didn't they start the album with this?

It's a good question. Both in song title and overall tone, it's this song that best captures the tension and edginess as the band took risks in the recording studio to try and create that album that would push their career to the next level. "*10-1* was the album that had to succeed," Hirst told Dodshon for his biography on the band.

"I remember walking around London with Jim and him saying 'I'm going to leave, the pressure's too much'. It was getting to everybody." It definitely got to Hirst, who famously had anxiety attacks during the recording of the album.

The song title interestingly leaves the last word unsaid. The phrase is "only the strong survive" but that final word is never mentioned in the lyrics. Whether intentional or not, it adds to the sense of despair and frustration apparent in the song, as though the protagonist really isn't sure they will survive all of this.

It's the soundtrack of the *10-1* process in four-and-half minutes (even the gentle end, where the band breathes a sigh of relief when the album's a success). So it's odd that the song was written a year before those stressful months in England in 1982. In his book *Willie's Bar and Grill*, Hirst vividly remembers where he was when he wrote it – which perhaps suggests *Only*

The Strong has some real resonance for him.

"There I am, back in 1981, sitting alone in the Diplomat Motor Inn in Acland Street, St Kilda, Melbourne," Hirst wrote.

"I'm going crazy in a room stinking of Winfields and Pine-o-Clean, with Chinese restaurant wallpaper all around and the remains of a fettuccine alfredo on the floor, scrawling the words to *Only The Strong*."

It turns out it's more a message of trying to survive life on the road and the endless touring the band was doing at the time. At least that's what he said in the DVD about the making of the album, also called *Only the Strong*. "It was a time when were doing gig after gig after gig," Hirst said.

"There was exhaustion, there was a road craziness and cabin fever going altogether [and being an asthmatic playing in venues that resembled "glorified ashtrays" didn't help].

"But it was really a case of just trying to survive that level of road work and making an impact live because there were so few waves anywhere else."

What's also odd is that, while the song sounds seamless (except perhaps for that acoustic pop chillout at the end) it's actually the result of a few different versions of the song combined to make the finished product.

For starters, that signature tremolo riff wasn't originally part of the song at all. Moginie was just pissfarting around in the rehearsal room when he played that. "Someone said we should put that in the song," he told *Depth Perception*, "just by itself. And you go 'what?!'. They you'd try it and it'd be great."

Hirst remembers those "urgent, breathy vocals" of Garrett weren't thought of until after the music was all recorded, the decision made following a band meeting over a dodgy curry at Shepherds Bush.

Then there's the drum track; Launay got Hirst to play the song through several times. Sometimes he'd play it straight, other times he could do his impression of Animal from *The Muppet Show*. Then Launay would cut out the best drum bits.

"I spent a whole day editing all the best bits together with razor blades and sticky tape," he told Divola, "but in the end that song to me captures what I saw live, where Midnight Oil is this powerful steamroller of a machine."

By Nick's own estimate, it took him 16 hours to reassemble all those bits of tape into a song.

Sixteen hours well-spent, I'd say

Short Memory
(Hirst/Moginie/Garrett)
3.53

Okay, so here's a story about a drunken bassplayer. The band had violinist Gisele Scales in to play on the song *Short Memory*, but no one knew quite what she going to play. Though it seemed the musical brainiac Moginie had a few ideas.

At that instant a drunken Peter Gifford stumbles into the studio and takes a seat at the back of the control room. After a while, as the drunk are prone to doing, Gifford is hit by what he believes is a genius idea; he knows exactly what Scales should play. So he heads out the studio, grabs her and explains his idea. Producer Launay lets Gifford have his moment, waiting for him to fall asleep in the corner and forget all about his violin-related moment of inspiration.

So Launay hits the 'record' button and Scales plays what Gifford has instructed. "And it's brilliant!" Launay remembers in Dodshon's *Beds Are Burning*. "It's what's on the record, it's totally him. That violin part on *Short Memory* is all his choice of notes." Gifford himself remembers he had a lot of input into the song, claiming ownership of the riff in the middle, the bass line and the whole groove.

Speaking of the bassplayer, it seems they're the most disposable member of Midnight Oil. It has been said the band couldn't continue with a new singer if Garrett left – indeed, when he quit to become a politician the rest of the guys didn't put another ad for a singer in the *Sydney Morning Herald*. And a Midnight Oil without Hirst on the kit? Not going to happen. It's the same for Moginie, who shares the heavy lifting when it comes to songwriting with Hirst. Rotsey? Well, he's the only member who actually looks like a rock god onstage, going hard with the guitar slinger moves to make up for the fact Moginie would perform as though someone taped a square metre of space on the stage and told him, "now don't bloody move out of that!" Rotsey has to be a part of any form of Midnight Oil.

But the bassplayer? Well, two of them have left and the band didn't seem to show any signs of thinking "well we can't go on without him. We'll have to call it a day". For me, Gifford is *the* Midnight Oil bassplayer. Bear James came and went before I knew the band so aside from the music, he was little more than a few blurry photos on album covers.

And Bones Hillman, well he may have been the bassplayer longer than the other two put together but, dammit, I can't help but see him as a session man brought in to replace the Big Giffo. The Oils image I carry in my head is of a hard-charging yet focused band. And that is Gifford – the man himself thinks so, telling biographer Dodshon he reckoned he helped shift the live dynamic to something harder, tougher and more driven. Perhaps your connection to one of the bassplaying trio is dependent on what period you discovered the band. Who knows, maybe there is a legion of US fans who think Hillman is the best bassplayer.

As for this song, it started out as a piece of Moginie's called *A Woman in History*. However, the experience of being in London and having an Irish Republican Army bomb explode a few blocks from where the band was staying while working on *10-1* changed it into a list of mankind's stupidity. Or, as Moginie puts it, "a list of these things people forget that happen again and again".

The Midnight Oil touring gallery exhibition in 2016-17 included a draft of the lyrics handwritten on a sheet of paper with the Gary Morris management letterhead. The first half of the finished song is basically the same as these early lyrics. It's the second half that's quite different. Those scrawled lyrics feature references to Reagan and El Salvador, Maggie Thatcher in The Falklands, the PLO, Idi Amin, Nazi Germany and the CIA.

Sonically, it's an eclectic piece. There are slight Indian influences (through guitars that sound like sitars), and the rhythm of the lyrics take in a drone-like quality which serves to emphasise the repetitive "these things keep on happening" idea which is at the root of the song.

Then, after the second chorus where a guitar solo would kick in, there's this odd sort-of guitar solo (which feels a bit like guitar noodling). Then the piano comes in and takes over, pushing the guitar to the background where it makes occasional sci-fi sounds. It goes for more than a minute and, if you really listen to it, sounds so very strange and yet it works in the broader context of the song.

Also worthy of note in the song is the reference to Hiroshima in the lyrics. It serves as a hint of what was to come; an album like *Red Sails in the Sunset*, where the fear of an approaching nuclear Armageddon is very much at the fore. But still, the mention of Hiroshima here suggests that fear was developing as far back as 1981 that a repeat of that horror of the morning of August 6, 1945, could happen again.

That morning, two planes flew over Hiroshima – one carrying a bomb called Little Boy and a second to monitor the effects once it was dropped. The Allies had chosen Hiroshima because it was an industrial centre, a key shipping port and the site of a major military headquarters. Also the city was surrounded by hills, which would amplify the effect of the bomb. It was one of five potential targets for the dropping of the first atomic bomb and, as such, had been spared from the traditional bombings suffered by other cities so the Allies could gain a full and accurate assessment of the devastation caused by the bomb.

The air raid sirens went off twice in Hiroshima that morning; the second time was when a plane flew over the city to check the weather and cloud coverage. An hour and 15 minutes later, the Enola Gay flew over the city – tragically the all-clear from the earlier air raid warning had sounded, meaning people had left cover and were now out in the streets.

At 8.15am the Enola Gay dropped its deadly cargo – actually 240 metres off target. Though that hardly matters with a bomb carrying the explosive force equivalent to 16 kilotonnes of TNT.

The residents of Hiroshima saw a blinding flash and then the firestorm. According to the account of journalist John Hershey "in a city of 245,000, nearly a 100,000 people had been killed or doomed with one blow".

He gives a horrific description of the countenances of those doomed souls; "their faces were wholly burned, their eye sockets were hollow, the fluid from their melted eyes had run down their cheeks. (They must have had their faces upturned when the bomb went off; perhaps they were anti-aircraft personnel). Their mouths were mere swollen, pus-covered wounds, which they could not bear to stretch enough to admit the spout of the teapot."

The burns from the flash made patterns in people's skin of undershirt straps and the flower patterns on the kimonos they wore. Hershey also wrote of the claim that numerous detailed human silhouettes had been burned into walls around the city, saying those claims had been overstated. Curiously, the blast heat cooked pumpkins on the vine and baked potatoes while still underground – survivors dug them out for sustenance.

Around 80,000 people – 30 per cent of the city's population – were killed in the blast and a further 70,000 injured. Incredibly, the Japanese military opted not to surrender; they figured the US could only have one or two more of these bombs and felt they would just endure those attacks and fight on.

So on August 9, another bomb-laden plane flew to Japan, bound for the city of Kokura. Smoke from the fires of a bombing raid in a nearby city obscured the target of Kokura, so the flight crew travelled to the second choice – Nagasaki.

At 10.53am the two B-29 Superfortresses were spotted but the air raid siren was not sounded as it was thought they were merely reconnaissance aircraft. Eight minutes later one of the planes dropped their bomb. While that bomb was more powerful than the one dropped on Hiroshima, the geography of Nagasaki limited the deadly nature of the blast. Between 35,000 and 40,000 people were killed immediately while 60,000 were injured. Tragically, around 200 people from Hiroshima had reportedly taken refuge in Nagasaki just before the bomb was dropped.

The Allies planned to have another bomb ready for August 19, and three more each in September and October. Fortunately for humanity, the Japanese

Emperor chose to surrender. To this day, despite constant fears of some crackpot regime launching nuclear weapons in a wartime setting, only one country has done that – the United States.

As a footnote for the song, a live performance of *Short Memory* appears in the rather odd 1984 film *One Night Stand*. Directed by John Duigan – an anti-nuke campaigner and friend of Peter Garrett – the film is available on YouTube and shows the band onstage at the Sydney Entertainment Centre.

The movie itself is best-described by Gemma Blackwood in a piece she wrote for The Conversation website. She saw it as "a teen comedy meets serious drama, which somehow seems to filter out the effectiveness of both of those genres". For all the nuclear war imagery, the movie ads in newspapers took an oddly lighthearted tone – "it's a nuclear war and they're having a blast!". In the interests of balance, *Sydney Morning Herald* movie reviewer Anna-Maria Dell'oso said at the time it "crosses the language of the rock clip with realism to produce an unnerving, amusing poignant and often embarrassingly honest film, a tense fantasy which teeters from raucousness to sobriety".

It's centred around four characters – two young female friends who work at the Sydney Opera House, a tradesman and a US sailor whose ship is docked in the harbour and who wants political asylum. Bombs drop on Europe and the US and, obeying the advice from a radio announcer, they all stay put inside the opera house. And go through the costume department and play dress-ups.

Soon bombs are dropped on Sydney. Ten minutes later, a character suggests they go outside because "the radiation would have died down now". For added protection, they take umbrellas out with them.

Seriously weird.

Read About It
(Hirst/Moginie/Garrett)
3.52

They were going to make Peter Garrett explode. Well, a Garrett dummy. The band were playing a gig at the Sidney Myer Music Bowl for Moomba in 1983. Someone got it into their head that it would be great if they rigged a dummy of Garrett to blow up while the band played *Read About It*.

Road crew boss Michael Lippold pointed the finger at manager Gary Morris in *Beds and Burning*, while Morris said it was someone else's idea. In the book *Pay to Play*, Garrett himself seemed rather keen on it, saying it was about putting across the idea that we were all just a push of a button away from being blown into a million pieces. But it was supposed to look like a soldier, not Garrett himself.

"We got the *Mad Max* stunt people in at great

expense, but they couldn't get it together to get us the 'soldier'," Garrett said. "So we got some sort of shop dummy which of course looked like me 'cos it didn't have any hair." And it apparently didn't go off properly either.

Lippold gave a fantastic three-page account of the incident to Dodshon. Garrett was to sneak offstage during the silent bit in the song and the roadie would creep onstage with the dummy, which would blow up and shock the crowd because they thought the lead singer had exploded. Only problem was the concert was at dusk so there was no way Lippold was going to be able to sneak onstage unseen – the jig would be up well before the faux Garrett went "kaboom!".

"I go out and put the fucking thing leaning up against the microphone," Lippold told Dodshon. "I'm not down low or anything, what's the point? I'm not invisible."

After having right the dummy after it fell over three times, Lippold had enough and started arguing with the explosives guy, telling him to push down on the plunger (or press a button, or whatever you do when you're trying to detonate a shop mannequin). It didn't blow up either, didn't come close; there was only a bit of smoke that came out, according to Lippold.

There was fireworks – well, fire actually – after a performance of *Read About It* on a US talk show a year later. In what may have been the band's first foray into the United States, they were booked on *Thicke of the Night* – hosted by one Alan Thicke (who played the dad on 1980s TV series *Growing Pains*, a show best known for giving Kirk Cameron his 15 minutes of fame as a pin-up for teenage girls).

It was a good gig; the band got to play three songs during the show (the other two were *Short Memory* and *Power & the Passion*). Despite the choice exposure, watching the footage on YouTube the band seems quite prickly during an interview with Thicke. Years later Hirst would tell the *Sydney Morning Herald*'s Bernard Zuel "we were kind of pissed off to be on the show for reasons I can't remember".

While interviewing Garrett, Thicke asks about his law degrees (which elicits a response of "not those questions again") and then the singer seems to mock the host for using the phrase "political or sociological sensitivity" and then there's the inevitable question about why they don't write love songs and a joke about how Garrett is so tall he should play basketball. I'd reckon if the band wasn't prickly before then having to run through the same obvious questions yet again might have made them that way.

Both this awkward interview and the live performance of *Read About It* can be found on YouTube. The band perform the song in a studio with the floor covered in newspaper – an idea of the band's, Hirst told Zuel, meant to portray "a raised middle finger to the quality of news in general". At least that's what they told the studio crew at *Thicke of the Night*. The real reason for the papers? So Garrett could set them on fire.

"He produced a match and the fire started burning quite vigorously by the time we finished the song," Hirst said to Zuel. "The stagehands all rushed out with fire extinguishers and the audience was absolutely aghast that they were going to be incinerated. We retreated in triumph to the back but they were not amused at all. No sense of humour."

Methinks Hirst is gilding the lily a bit here. The video on YouTube shows Garrett picking up a newspaper page just before the pause in the song. He pulls a lighter out of the breast pocket of his overalls and lights up the page. When the fire catches hold, he drops it on the floor on top of the other papers. Around 10 seconds later someone (it very much looks like road crew boss Lippold) runs onstage and seems to be putting out the flame before carrying away a stack of papers. At the same time Rotsey looks to be trying to stamp out the fire.

And that's it. No more flames. But, really, the idea that the fire burned until the end of the song is ludicrous. Remember, the band and all their equipment is standing on top of these papers; if the paper kept burning through the last minute of the song, then it would have surely burnt the band too.

Hirst may not be the best at telling a story, but jeez he's a dab hand at writing. I mean, just check out the first line in this song, about the rich, the poor and the picture. It's just nine words long but it speaks volumes about the disparity and inequality in society and how one side doesn't care about those less fortunate and the other side knows they're not going to be able to do much of anything about it. They can be as meek as they want but there's no way they're inheriting anything. And, as an added bonus, the damn line rhymes.

In Debbie Kruger's excellent book *Songwriters Speak*, Hirst said lyric writing was so often not a pleasure. "In the majority of cases I would spend ages on them," he told Kruger, "until I found something that in some way seemed to me something just beautifully put."

Well that first line is so beautifully put that I'm pretty sure that when Hirst wrote it, he must have sat back and admired the genius of it and then chose to put his feet up for the rest of the day. If I'd just written a line like that I'd be damn sure to rest on my laurels for at least a day.

But even before that first line, what do we have? A cowbell – man there isn't a song on Earth that can't be improved by some cowbell. Not hard to figure out a drummer wrote this song. It was so significant to Hirst he made sure to mention it in a track-by-track overview accompanying the release of the compilation album *Flat Chat*.

"I sang the words and melody of this one to Jim in the sunny lounge room of his first home in Putney, down by the Parramatta River," Hirst said.

"Jim strummed along, adding the crunchy riff which, propelled by a relentless cowbell, later anchored the song to solid rock." Yet in the *Only the Strong* doco Moginie reckoned that riff didn't surface until one night in the band's share house in London's St John's Wood. "I remember staying up all night one night and the guitar riff at the beginning popped out," he said.

The song itself takes a swipe at the media, claiming there's all this important stuff going on and yet it never makes the papers (you could mount a case for the song being even more pertinent today). It flips the phrase "you wouldn't read about it" on its ear too. Traditionally said in reference to something unbelievable or amazing, here the phrase takes on a more basic meaning – these stories, these issues? You're just not going to read about them.

It marked a bit of a change in lyrical focus for the band. "It was fairly political in its nature," Moginie told the *Only The Strong* documentary, "and we hadn't really been writing those kinds of songs before."

For the video the band headed off to Jenolan Caves to film in the Devil's Coach House Cave, just near the entrance (in a number of shots you can see the entrance in the background, along with the path and stairs tourists take when traipsing through the cave). Early on Rob Hirst does something you only ever see drummers do in music videos – dance around hitting his sticks together. I would bet you no drummer has ever done that at any other time. It's like a director says "okay band, I need you to all dance around so I can get a few shots".

That works fine for the guitarists, who have their instrument slung over their shoulder, and the singers – well, they're just dancing. But the drummer, well, the director wants viewers to *know* they're the drummer, so they make the poor sap to hold their drumsticks while they dance around and bang them together like a kid in pre-school. It always looks naff. Always. Though perhaps not as naff as Garrett tucking the ends of his overalls into his black socks like he's about to get on a pushbike and cycle home after the shoot.

But the real head-scratcher? The guitars of Moginie and Rotsey. Some of the guitar work on *Read About It* sounds acoustic but during those parts of the video the pair are seen playing electric guitars. Weird.

Scream in Blue
(Rotsey/Moginie/Garrett)
6.22

"How come you don't write any love songs?" During the band's rise in the United States that seemed to be a question they were asked over and over again. And it wasn't until the Americans started asking that I'd even realised the lack of love songs. Up to that point it had never mattered to me that they weren't singing about some old girlfriend they had in high school or some hot woman they just spotted across the club and how they planned to go and chat her up.

Some bands just sang songs about love, others didn't – at the end of the day they're all just singing about what's important to them.

And maybe Midnight Oil, you know, kind of sucked when it came to writing songs about falling in love.

"Well I think we realised early on that our strengths weren't to write love songs," Moginie, one of the band's two main songwriters, explained to the *Observer*'s John Kruth. "That was well covered by others. People like The Clash, Woody Guthrie, Phil Ochs, Skyhooks, Cold Chisel were writing about real life, the latter two with a proudly Australian bent. They made us realize that songs could be about something, not be-bop-alula or soppy commercial fodder, but inspirational, and that could connect us to a potential audience who wanted something with a bit of flesh and blood and not saccharine."

Hirst, the other main songwriter, would agree with that assessment. "Some people write great love songs," Hirst told the *LA Times*' Mike Boehm. "It's not something that we've been able to do convincingly because of the preoccupations of the main writers."

Those preoccupations seem to include serious political issues, which is what so many of the songs are about. At least that's the impression many people have about Midnight Oil songs, which is frustrating for the songwriters themselves.

"No one would be in any way interested in what we were saying politically," Hirst told Boehm, "unless there were some killer melodies and good rhythms where you could move your feet."

It's a statement Moginie agrees with, going so far as to tell Debbie Kruger that interviewers throwing endless political questions at the band really got on his wick. He'd tell them "it's just a bloody band", only to have other members say "hey, it's more than 'just a band'."

"Well, if it doesn't work as a band, it just doesn't work," he told Kruger. "It doesn't matter how many messages you want to whack on top, if the band part of it is no good and the songs are no good, no-one's going to want to listen to it."

They're right, you know. You hear a great song on the radio, it's not the lyrics that grab you first. It's the music. The music bypasses the rational areas of your brain and burrows its way into your emotional side. It's only after that point any message in the lyrics gets any attention from the listener. Music is the Trojan horse that gets the words past the gatekeeper.

Anyway, the word "love" *has* appeared in a few Midnight Oil songs. It pops up in the chorus of *Blue Sky Mining*'s *Shakers and Movers* but the chorus is about mercenary real estate developers – so that's a bit confusing. And to me the line with love in it sounds a bit leaden when it comes out of Garrett's mouth. There's *Outbreak of Love* from *Earth and Sun and Moon*, though songwriter Hirst has said that's about the end of a relationship, about the absence of love.

Another apparent starter is the apostrophe-challenged *Loves on Sale* from *Place Without a Postcard*. Though reading the lyrics, it seems more like a song about rampant consumerism – it's more about what material goods your heart desires rather that any desire for another human being.

What appears to be the most obvious love song is *Head Over Heels*, from their debut. But it's not hard to also interpret the lyrics as telling the tale of frustration with the fickle nature of fans who liked the band in the early days but then gave up on them as they grew in popularity (though the idea of popularity was relative, given *Head Over Heels* came from their first album).

It's *Scream in Blue* which is the band's most overt love song – though you need to wait until it's one-third over before reaching the "love" bit. Unlike the love line in *Shakers and Movers*, there's nothing leaden in Garrett's delivery. Accompanied by a piano line and Gifford's double bass (though some guitar and thunder-like drums come in near the end) I can imagine that he has his then-partner now-wife Doris on his mind when he sings it.

But you wonder if the band is a little worried about having it on the album, because they've effectively hidden it behind two-and-a-bit minutes of sometimes discordant hurdy gurdy "Beatles circa *Revolver*" skyrocket music. Well, at least that's what it sounds like to me.

That Garrett ballad at the end is the best part of the song, and yet it's that part of the song that gets chopped when it appears on the band's live album. An album which takes its name from that song. One assumes the reason is that slow bit doesn't really fit the purpose of that live album.

The Oils broke into the big time on the back of what – to my ears at least – are the band's two most commercial-sounding albums. Both *Diesel and Dust* and *Blue Sky Mining* saw the band move away from their intense rock character and towards songs with more of a pop-rock feel. That was helpful, until the early 1990s when grunge came along and turned the music industry upside-down.

And there was Midnight Oil with its poppy sound climbing up the charts, looking at these kids with long hair and flannelette shirts. Perhaps the Oils thought "we rocked harder than these kids ages ago". And they'd be right – put the late '70s-early'80s Oils onstage alongside any grunge-era band you care to name and the Australian fivepiece wipes the floor with them. Yes, even that band with the Foo Fighters guy on drums. But this massive new audience they've created only knew them for stuff like *Beds Are Burning* (let's face it, it's only hardcore music lovers who, upon discovering a new band, go and check out their back catalogue).

There was only one thing for it – release a live album. An album where just five of the 12 tracks come from those two huge-selling albums. An album that says "hey, we're not just a band with acoustic guitars and bush hats". An album that shows the band can smash it out. An album that shows their back catalogue includes a load of songs that compel you to turn up the volume on the stereo.

That tender Garrett section at the back end of *Scream in Blue* just didn't fit into the game plan so the live version was chopped out just before we got to it. Which is rather a pity.

Side Two
US Forces
(Moginie/Garrett)
4.06

It seems Gifford was responsible for the band's overalls, according to Andrew Stafford's liner notes to the *Overflow Tank* compilation. "The arrival of Peter Gifford had given the band a harder look too, including work-wear overalls that several members would soon adopt," Stafford wrote. Whether true or not, overalls very much fit the Gifford "I'm here to work, not arse about" attitude that hardened Midnight Oil and, I reckon, was part of what got them over the hump and into the next stage of their career.

And, look, if I'm being totally honest, the rest of the band couldn't really pull off the overall look. Just check out the video for *US Forces* – shot at Vales Point power station on the NSW Central Coast. Four of the members are sporting the new look (Garrett has opted for street clothes and a hoodie) and it's only Gifford who looks like he's ever worn overalls before. In fact, I wouldn't be surprised if they're the very same overalls he wore while working as a carpenter before joining the band.

So what about the rest of the band? There's Hirst wearing what looks like a brand-spanking new set in bright blue, trying to look cool with his collar up. Rotsey's in grey, a poorly chosen colour as he so often blends into the dark background. And Moginie, well he must have been last to wardrobe because he got stuck with an awful purple number and he looks even more awkward than usual. Maybe that's why he so seldom appears in the video. All bar one of his appearances are in a wide shot of the whole band. Even Hirst appears more than Moginie; I like drummers, but on what Earth does a drummer get more close-ups than a guitarist?

The song was the first single, released in November 1982, a month ahead of the *10,9,8,7,6,5,4,3,2,1* album itself. It was written largely by Moginie, who says that first line came straight from a newspaper headline. That may well be the case but a search of online newspaper archives both in Australia and England (where the song was recorded) throws up no such headline. Not that it matters - I just mention this to illustrate the depths I went to in researching this book.

The song seems oddly named, taking the title from its first two words – words that are never uttered again. That's because *US Forces* wasn't the original title; producer Launay said the name in the studio was *The Next Big Thing*. As soon as he brought it to their attention that radio DJs would say "here's the next big thing from Midnight Oil" the band changed their mind.

In choosing to rename it *US Forces*, it seemed to be another instance of the band's bloody-mindedness. A title like that seemed destined to play poorly across vast swathes of America, which was a place the album was meant to reach. But, no, no, no Moginie said in the *Kings of the Mountain* doco for Music Max, it wasn't meant that way at all.

"I think '*US Forces* give the nod' was a sentiment that a lot of Americans took the wrong way," he said. "They were 'how dare you insult us when we saved you in the Second World War'. The point was that they were taking over the world by owning it with money, coming into countries and taking over like that.

"I love American people but the politics of America has been a bit of a problem. The same sentiments are still going on 35 years later."

While he was in federal politics, Garrett saw that song very differently – as he would given he was part of a government that supported the Pine Gap defence facility (the very same facility he criticised as Midnight Oil frontman). For him, *US Forces* was most definitely NOT meant to be a reflection of anything "still going on 35 years later".

"It's a song of its time," he told *Rolling Stone*'s Barry Divola in 2012. "It was about what we as a country were facing in terms of the stand-off between the United States and the Soviet Union.

"It's hard to put yourself back in that place now and remember how the Cold War atmosphere was such a big concern and how potentially dangerous it was. That is the essence of the song."

When it comes to what we hear on the song itself, there are two stories that are told most often. There's the one about being out of tune and the one about the piano strings.

Out of Tune: The story goes that the band worked up all the sounds we hear into a complete whole before Garrett went in to record his bit. But they worked out rather quickly that it wasn't working for him, because they'd recorded it in the wrong key for his voice. So they were going to have to start all over again.

They dropped this bombshell on Launay, who was the very opposite of chuffed. He eventually managed to take most of the song and, via studio trickery, get it to the right key without having to re-record the whole thing. Except for the intro, which various band members have said makes it sound slightly odd when Garrett comes in because it's in two different keys. It must be a musician thing because there's nothing jarring about that bit to me at all; perhaps because there's a gap of a few seconds before Garrett sings the first line.

The Piano Strings: This one is actually a neat story. In the chorus, there's this odd sound; like a cross between a hurdy-gurdy on a carousel and a kids' toy. That's Hirst hitting strings on a piano with his sticks. The strings he wasn't supposed to hit were covered in gaffer tape, though that would have hardly made it much easier. He was asked to play a really fast beat and he would have had to play it properly too.

At the risk of alienating people, let me nail my colours to the mast. I don't like *US Forces*. Didn't like it back in the 1980s when I was a teenager and I still don't like it now. Other songs on *10,9,8* I disliked in my younger days but my older self has developed an appreciation for (hello, *Somebody's Trying to Tell Me Something*), but this one? Nope. I find it both too poppy and the least interesting song on the album; it was never going to be "the next big thing" as far as I was concerned.

Power & The Passion
(Hirst/Moginie/Garrett)
5.39

The band weren't the greatest fans of the disco era – in late 1979 they headlined several gigs under the "Death to Disco" banner. At one of those gigs thousands of disco records were reportedly set on fire. Hirst had a particular dislike of that style of music, and reggae as well, as he told music writer Stuart Coupe that year.

"As a drummer I find disco rhythms very limiting," he said. "And the same can be said for reggae. Rock 'n' roll covers, from a rhythmical point of view, a huge number of styles and complexities but both disco and reggae are locked into a single beat which you play all night. You slow it down and speed it up, but it's just like a tape loop. You might as well record two bars and just repeat it."

And yet just a few years later, Hirst would be playing on a disco song, most of which was a single beat, and it would end up being the band's biggest hit to date and the first to crack the top 10 singles charts.

The irony wasn't lost on the band during the recording. Moginie certainly saw the ridiculousness of *this* band doing *that* sort of song. "It was a bit of a joke," he said in the Music Max doco *The Artist's Story*. "'Let's do a disco song'. That's how that song came into being, as a bit of a joke. We were just laughing when we were making it, thinking 'this is ridiculous'."

Hirst himself was struggling to find the humour in the 'disco' song. That was partially because, while in London, he was suffering from what he later realised was a nervous breakdown. It was also because Launay wanted him to use the then-brand new LinnDrum, which was a drum machine that used real drum sounds and which was being used by bands instead of a flesh-and-blood drummer.

Today, using samples in a song isn't anything to worry about but in the early days of drum machines there was a genuine fear these contraptions would end up replacing drummers (though can you seriously imagine Midnight Oil with a drum machine up the back?). On top of that, a drummer being asked to play on the same song as a drum machine would have felt like a bit of an insult, as though it was being suggested that they could not play that part better than the machine.

"Nick also introduced the band to drum machines, which I was really resistant to at the time," Hirst said in *The Artist's Story*. "There was a thing then about being a drummer or a nerd, but you couldn't combine the two.

"Sequencers and samplers were thought of as a major threat to drummers all over the world."

What else contributed to Hirst's angst over this song was the fact that Garrett changed his lyrics. Hirst and Moginie had worked it up together into a recordable song (though Gifford remembers the song took a lot of jamming to bring the song together) but, Launay said in *Beds Are Burning*, Garrett would secretly change the lyrics and not reveal them until the last minute.

"What he often did, which was kind of disrespectful to Rob or Jim, was write new lyrics and not discuss them at all," Launay said. "He would have them, no one had seen them, and when he went out to do the vocal he would just sing his lyrics – and with *Power & The Passion* his lyrics completely ignored Rob's lyrics."

Garrett said he didn't remember anything unusual about Hirst's reaction, which does sound like a bit of spin on the singer's part. Hirst himself hinted at a sense of frustration over this to Kruger in her book *Songwriters Speak*. Talking about that sort-of-rap Garrett flings off about Pine Gap, Big Mac and old women's blue-rinse hairdos. Hirst admitted to Kruger it "made the song fantastic" but mentioned Garrett's work on that song followed a pattern of last-minute changes, when the producer virtually had their finger hovering over the "record" button. "Almost always delivered at the nth hour," Hirst said of the changes. "I would sometimes dread coming into the studio because it was just so fraught."

There was also a second, lesser-known piece of Garrett improvisation in *Power & The Passion* – over that iconic drum solo. The *Only The Strong* DVD plays a few samples of the riffs, which included very Australian phrases like "let's get the bus to Manly" and "there's a knock in the diesel engine". It didn't make the finished product – which may have been a little fortunate as having Garrett adlib over Hirst's big moment in that song might well have pushed the drummer right over the edge.

That solo wasn't just Hirst's big moment, it's arguably *the* moment in *Power and The Passion*. It's certainly the moment that is talked about the most – even if that talk is somewhat contradictory. To deal with his panic attacks Hirst has said he would go out on long runs to work off some energy and stress; "to try and get myself straight". In one version of the story he has told, Hirst came straight in after one of those runs and went at it on the kit for that drum solo. Other times he's said he opted *not* to go for a run on the day he was recording it so as to harness all that stress and direct it at his kit.

Then there's the "full stop" at the end of the solo – the smashing of a big light bulb. Hirst said he picked it up at the end of the solo and, on the spur of the moment, hurled it at the wall. That never really seemed possible to me, because the smashing globe is heard on the track almost at the same time as Hirst's final beat of a drumroll. I just can't see how a drummer – even one as undoubtedly talented as Hirst – could play a drumroll with two hands and pick up a light globe at the same time and throw it at a wall.

In the biography *Beds Are Burning* Launay suggests a different and more satisfactory version of events. In stating the drum solo was recorded first-take, the producer said "the only thing we added was that breaking sound that finished it." That was achieved by Hirst dropping it on the stone floor of the drum room.

That clearly suggests the smash of the globe was an overdub rather than something recorded during the drum solo itself.

When it comes to the *10-1* album, this is *the* song from the album. It gave the band their first top 10 single in Australia – hitting No8. And it's one of the most recognisable from their whole career. I'd say it's *Beds Are Burning* in first place and this song in second spot. To its credit *Power & The Passion* has managed to avoid the contempt that comes with that sort of familiarity. Let's face it, there are plenty of songs that sounded great when we first heard them but get played so many damn times we get heartily sick of them. Few things can kill the joy of a song by hearing it too many times.

Nirvana's *Smells Like Teen Spirit* comes to mind – loved it back them but hearing it so many times over the years has totally deadened any joy I once got from the song. I hear it now and I do an internal eye roll and think "oh great, It's *this* song. Again."

That feeling doesn't accompany *Power & The Passion*. I'll take a punt and say it's because there's so much going on that you can keep finding something new. For instance, it wasn't until recently that I noticed all the bass noodling Gifford does at the back end, under those ever-rising horns. Man, I loved those horns for so long but now, when I listen to this song, what do I hear at the back end? Yep, Gifford taking his bass for a walk around the fretboard. There's so much other stuff going on here; a little maraca-like sound that accompanies the drumbeats, some electric drum sampling, a little noise I can only describe as a "twinkle" just after the line about skin that's so brown.

Even some things that aren't going on add to the song. Like the relative lack of guitar. Midnight Oil is a band with not one, but two guitarists, but there are plenty of stretches in the song where there's no guitar at all. And then even when they do come it, it's as though they're taking a back seat to the drums and bass; "okay, those guys are driving this song, let's stay out of their way".

Even that drum solo, where the attention is on Hirst, Gifford is laying down a funky groove behind it – which you don't really notice until you go looking for it. It's the drum and bass combo that made the 12-inch remix of this track (apparently reworked by Francois Kervorkian, who would go onto produce the *Species Deceases* EP) so good. There's a really great groove and swing here that the Oils weren't previously known for.

The video for the song has become just as iconic as the song itself – though it did spark some controversy. Filmed under the Eastern Distributor in the rather vowel-heavy inner Sydney suburb of Woolloomooloo, it featured the band performing in front of a memorable mural that bore the phrase "I love a plundered country … a land of corporate gains" (an alteration of the Dorothea MacKellar poem *My Country*).

That mural perfectly reflected the stance of Midnight Oil and it may seem as though it was painted for the video. But it – and six others – were there first as part of the 1982 Woolloomooloo Mural Project created as a protest against the intensive development that was happening in the area at the time. According to a detailed piece by Kris Swales for theMusic.com.au, there was some conflict between the band and those behind the mural project.

"We had a real run-in with Midnight Oil at the time because they didn't ask our permission to shoot in front of the murals," said curator Merilyn Fairskye. "We were really heavily involved with the beginning of the Artworkers Union and with artists' rights to control the way in which their works would be used."

She said the band eventually paid the two artists Grahame Kime and Robin Hicks a $50 usage fee. Video director Ray Argall – who said the band would have gotten permission to film there from the local council – pointed out in the article the budget for the entire video would have been less than $5000.

It could well have been Gifford's idea to film there; in the *Kings of the Mountain* documentary Garrett said the bassist was living near the murals. "Then Peter Gifford … was living in a squat around the corner from Woolloomooloo. We just decided to set up under the flyover in front of the concrete that had all the graffiti on it." In terms of Giffo's squat I presume he means the buildings the band perform in front of right at the start of the video rather than the murals that dominate it.

The video was shot in two parts – the first was the live performance in front of the murals. Argall said they did four run-throughs of the song. The next day the band came back and played a few more versions so Argall could get that footage we see of the band in an onscreen 'box' during the second half of the video. That's where there's a continuity gaffe as several members of the band are wearing different clothes from the night before.

There's another continuity issue as well during the period where Hirst starts chucking his drumkit off that large wooden box. At one stage he kicks the whole thing off the makeshift drum riser, then a few seconds later the camera cuts back to Hirst who is magically on top of that box playing a full kit again.

There was another little jab at *Countdown* in the *Power & The Passion* video, according to the US website NightFlight. In 2017 Bryan Thomas wrote a retrospective on the band to coincide with their reunion and world tour.

In that piece Thomas pointed to the numerous company logos and signs that flash through the video. Thomas said the band purposely added the logos and emblems to make it impossible for *Countdown* – which aired on the non-commercial, government-owned ABC network – to screen the video.

Maralinga
(Moginie/Garrett)
4.44

These days, it's hard to imagine the Australian Prime Minister answering "yes" to the question, "hey, can we explode atomic bombs in your country?". You just can't fathom it, can you? And yet that's just what renowned Anglophile Robert Menzies did when the British came calling in the years after World War II. The year after the war, nuclear cooperation between the US and Britain ended and so the Brits saw the need to build up its own arsenal of bombs.

Part of that involved testing them – to make sure they worked, I guess – and so they fished around for someone who would let them do that. Canada with its big empty spaces looked like a goer. The Canucks got cold feet when they realised the British wanted to carry out at least a dozen tests, each of which would contaminate a new 450-metre diameter circle.

So come on down Robert Menzies, who had been elected to his second stint as Australian Prime Minister on December 19, 1949. And it took just a phone call for him to allow the British scientists to explode big, deadly things on our soil. British PM Clement Attlee rang in September 1950 and asked if Menzies would be cool with that. He was *totally* cool with that, so cool that he didn't even see the need to run it by his Cabinet, scientists or anybody else. The English had come calling and Menzies was always willing to help the English; despite being born in Australia he saw himself as a British subject.

It's a decision that seems quite odd, given the Second World War had ended with the explosion of not one but two atomic bombs and, by the 1950s, the human carnage they caused was well-known. In her book *Atomic Thunder*, academic Elizabeth Tynan, suggests it wasn't just Menzies being weird – the world of the 1950s had a much rosier view of atomic weapons.

"His enthusiasm for nuclear testing was not considered strange at the time," Tynan wrote. "Despite the initial shock at the destruction of Hiroshima and Nagasaki, many people in the West saw atomic weaponry and energy as positive and forward-looking developments."

While the name Maralinga is known to many as the site of atomic testing, it was actually the third location the British used to test bombs. In October 1952, they tested a nuclear weapon at the Monte Bello Islands, 130 kilometres off the coast of Western Australia. Called Operation Hurricane, it featured a bomb housed in a ship's hull that sat 2.7 metres below the waterline. The detonation was deemed a success of sorts; while the test showed the bomb design worked, it had been in a boat which was not going to be the preferred method of delivery to the target. That would be via a plane, so more tests were needed.

Those extra tests ended up being conducted at Emu Field in South Australia, around 200 kilometres north of Maralinga. Two bombs – each attached to a tower – were detonated there on separate dates in October 1953. Tagged Operation Totem, the first explosion generated so much heat it turned the soil at the bomb site into glass. The second pushed an 8500-metre mushroom cloud into the sky and the explosion was felt hundreds of kilometres away.

By this time, the secrecy Menzies adopted with the first tests had disappeared. Stories of the Emu Field blasts actually appeared in Australian newspapers at the time. Here's how the *Wagga Daily Advertiser* described that second explosion:

"The tower was vaporised, and the red desert country for a radius of five miles was swept up in the blast. Three minutes after the firing, the familiar mushroom cloud sitting on top of a long, elegant neck of smoke, ironically took on the profile of an aborigine [sic] staring over his native land. In five minutes the cloud had reached the maximum peak of 15,000 feet and immediately a Canberra jet bomber dived through the cloud to sample radioactivity."

Melbourne Herald journalist WS Noble got a close-up – and likely cancer-causing – view of Ground Zero. "An hour after the blast I was allowed to fly over the spot where the blast had been fired. All that remained was a fire-blackened circle. It looked as if the ground itself had taken fire. Wisps of smoke rose from where the tower had been."

The remoteness of Emu Field meant it was hard to get infrastructure to the test site. So the British asked for and got yet more Australian soil to contaminate – Maralinga. After a while, those tests would be closed to the media as the public began to oppose the idea of bombs going off and the very real risk of fallout being blown by the wind across population centres. The location was announced in May 1955, after the Australian government, keen to look less like the bit player we really were in this deal, offered to pay some of the costs of the test site. This was even after Britain had said it was prepared to pay for everything.

A secret Cabinet document from 1954 (by this time Menzies was sharing some information with his ministers) said Australia offered to pick up "the cost of Australian personnel engaged in the preparation of the site, and of materials and equipment which could be recovered after the tests, should fall to Australia's account". The British were okay with that, why wouldn't they be?

When the first tests moved to Maralinga, the upbeat view of atomic bombs hadn't changed. Some papers even saw fit to make light of it. A story in the *Melbourne Argus* in June told of an atomic bomb being dropped on the site – in the form of a woman.

"The atomic bomb was slim, grey-eyed, 24-year-old air hostess Nan Whitcome, formerly of Elsternwick. Most of the 1600 men in this womanless area hadn't seen a woman for six months."

The story was headlined 'A blonde bombshell blew up Maralinga'. The use of the test site's name in the headline suggests both it and what was happening there was well-known to Australians at the time.

The first mushroom cloud over the 3200 square-kilometre Maralinga test site occurred on September 27, 1956. It was the first in a series of trials tagged Operation Buffalo. Both it and Buffalo 4 were detonated from towers, Buffalo 3 was dropped from a plane and no2 was exploded at ground level.

The *Canberra Times* covered the blast, the first words of the front-page story reading "A Hiroshima-sized atomic bomb exploded on Maralinga …". Given the significance of the moment – the first Maralinga blast – this is how the *Times* correspondent saw things.

"The steel tower nestling the bomb was vaporised except for some red-hot fragments scattered over the range.

"The fireball, a white-hot mass, expanded into a gigantic bubble. All minerals and rock in the tower area were fused by the intense heat as the air heated to incandescence.

"A second or two after the explosion, the fireball shot upwards as it lost its intensity it continued to expand with a brilliant orange glow.

"As the fireball swept upwards, explosive gases swirled up, forming the head of a mushroom and earth sucked up by the fireball formed the stem of the mushroom.

"Ten seconds after the explosion the top of the cloud turned snow-white. A plume of radioactive dust fell from the cloud as it began to move up the mainland."

By this time there had been a change in public opinion, due to a pair of bomb tests back at the Monte Bello Islands in mid-1956. The second test, named Mosaic G2, was and remains the biggest A-bomb unleashed on Australian soil – almost 100 kilotonnes (the bomb dropped on Hiroshima was just 15 kilotonnes). The cloud from the explosion rose 14,000 metres and spread across the continent. The public had been told the explosion would be small, so seeing such a large cloud caused fears that something had gone dreadfully wrong.

And further tests at Maralinga didn't allay their feelings. There were six more bomb tests at Maralinga through to October 1957 – four under Operation Buffalo and three under Operation Antler. After Antler, to limit what the public knew about the testing the media was shut out of Maralinga.

This was unfortunate, given that the really dangerous experiments at the test site were about to begin. Ironically named "minor trials" and given innocuous code names like Kittens and Vixen, they were what Tynan classed the "most damaging activities from the 11 years of British nuclear testing in Australia".

These tests were designed to see what would happen in the event of an accidental explosion of an A-bomb en route to its destination. For instance, what would happen if a plane carrying a bomb crash-landed? To find out they used TNT to blow up simulated warheads containing plutonium.

What these experiments did was scatter more than 22 kilograms of a particularly heinous form of plutonium across the South Australian desert. During a less-than-enthusiastic clean-up by the British, some of this was buried, some of it wasn't, and then the Brits told Australia everything was sweet and left.

When Midnight Oil recorded *Maralinga*, the depths of British deceit and the dangers of the tests were being uncovered. It started in 1978 when investigative journalist Brian Toohey got hold of a secret Cabinet document about plutonium buried at Maralinga. The document expressed fears that a group of terrorists could go there and simply dig up some of it. "They could then threaten, say, to exploit the extremely toxic properties of plutonium against the population of a major city," the document said.

By 1984, the Hawke government set up the McClelland Royal Commission into the tests. The resulting findings would condemn pretty much every aspect of the tests and initiate a process to clean up the area at a cost of $108 million.

Another shocking aspect of the British tests was the casual disregard for human safety.

Soldiers were used as guinea pigs during the Maralinga blasts, though they were officially called the Indoctrinee Force. A 60-40 split between British and Australian troops, they were placed less than nine kilometres from Ground Zero to see what happened to them. "The world was facing the real prospect of nuclear war, and the Indoctrinees were ordered to report back to their military colleagues what the future had in store," Tynan wrote.

For his book *Maralinga*, Frank Walker spoke to numerous soldiers present at the tests. Leading Aircraftsman Ric Johnstone was at the Buffalo tests and it was his job to go into the "hot zone" just after the explosion to gather equipment. He recalled being told to put the palms of his hands into his eye sockets before the blast, and noticed it was so bright he could see the bones of his hands. Out in the hot zone, he said the protective gear was awful – they couldn't breathe through the masks or work with the thick rubber gloves. So they just took it all off.

Walker also stated some soldiers were required to see just how contaminated they could get. "One group sat in the back of a truck as it raced around the blast area stirring up as much dust as possible, the second was ordered to march through the area and brush up against bushes and trees while a third was ordered to roll around the dust for 50 metres and crawl through the brush for another 50."

The Midnight Oil song *Maralinga* is told from the point of view of the Aboriginal population's direct experience of the blasts. As early as 1957 the British were trying to wipe their hands of any responsibility for whatever happened to the Aboriginal population. In the House of Commons, the Under-Secretary for Commonwealth Relations was asked about claims Aboriginal people were taken away from their tribal grounds. "These are not our bomb testing grounds," he said. "The problem there must be dealt with by the Australian government." So while the bombs were British, any blame was Australia's.

Years later the McClelland Royal Commission found both governments were at fault – neither cared much for the safety of the Aboriginal population. "If Aborigines were not injured or killed as a result of the explosions, this is a matter of luck rather than adequate organisation, management and resources allocated to ensuring safety," the commissioner found.

The Royal Commission also found that, unbelievably, the sum total of research into the

Aboriginal population carried out ahead of the early tests was a single paper that heavily relied on the Encylopaedia Britannica. A number of witnesses to the Royal Commission also reported seeing Aboriginal men, women and children within the "forbidden zone".

Perhaps the most high-profile incident involving the Aboriginal people and the effects of the British tests is "the black mist". Australian musician Paul Kelly wrote *Maralinga (Rainy Land)* about the incident, though it actually happened at Emu Field and not Maralinga.

A number of Aboriginal people were on a cattle homestead around 170 kilometres away when the first Totem test was conducted at Emu Field. They reported hearing a loud bang but thought nothing more of it. Then, the next day, a black, greasy mist rolled in.

"It was coming from the south," Yami Lester, who was 11 at the time of the blast, told the Royal Commission, "black-like smoke. I was thinking it might be a dust storm, but it was quiet, just moving … through the trees and above that again, you know. It was just rolling and moving quietly."

He said everything went dark and people began to panic, digging holes for protection against the mist. It felt sticky on his skin and he could hear a slight hiss as it settled all around him.

The next day, people began to get sick; vomiting, stinging eyes, skin rashes. Then they began dying – estimates vary from 12 to around 40. In his teens, Lester would go blind – and he would be convinced it was the fault of the black mist. The same black mist that killed the others.

Because the black mist was atomic fallout.

Tin-Legs & Tin Mines
(Rotsey/Moginie/Garrett)
4.28

There are a few songs on *10,9,8,7,6,5,4,3,2,1* that the band knew were going to mess with people's heads. The album opener *Outside World* was one and the disco banger that is *Power & The Passion* was another.

I do wonder a little whether *Tin-Legs & Tin Mines* was also created in that same vein. "Hey, let's write a song with a whole lot of random phrases that don't really mean anything when they're all strung together and watch as people go crazy trying to work out what the song's about."

Of all the songs on *10-1*, this would have to be the most impenetrable and the least-discussed. It doesn't get a mention in the band bio *Beds Are Burning*, nor does anyone talk about in either of the two documentaries about the making of the making of *10-1*. Not even Michael Lawrence's hardback on the band – which is a wealth of Midnight Oil minutiae – offers any indication on just what their stance was when it came to either tin legs or tin mines.

In my research I was able to find just three instances where a band member talks about the song. One of those is Rob Hirst, via a 1984 interview with Bill Wolfe for a drum magazine. When asked for songs that best represent his drumming, he said there are two extremes – one where the drums are up back of the songs and others where they're right up the front. *Tin-Legs & Tin Mines* is an example of the latter, "where the choruses are actually propelled by the drumbeat."

The second instance appears on a bonus interview disc that was released with the band's less-than-necessary CD *The Real Thing*. I had to track down a copy via eBay, spending more than I probably should have in the hope that, because the song appears on the main disc, the band might talk about it on the interview disc (which was for radio stations to play so they could trick listeners into thinking they'd actually spoken to the band).

It would have been great if, on that disc, a band member would spill their guts about *Tin-Legs*, the scales would fall away from my eyes and I would be illuminated by the knowledge. Nope, didn't happen. All I got for my eBay purchase was Garrett talking about how, when it comes to performing songs you don't play all that often, they jog memories for you when they appear on the setlist.

"When you come to it you're thinking 'Oh, okay, here are the words, this is why this song was written, this is what we were feeling at the time'."

In a way that was worse than if they didn't mention the song at all. He's actually talking about how playing *Tin-Legs & Tin Mines* brought back all these memories about the origins of the song, but declines to actually explain what those origins are. If I didn't know better, I'd say he was teasing me.

The third mention – in the *Full Tank* liner notes – is just as frustrating. And it's also from Garrett. Journalist Sean Sennett stated the subject matter of *Red Sails in the Sunset* is "the broad church of politics, militarism, the seemingly very real threat of nuclear war, consumerism and environmental issues".

Then in the next paragraph, Garrett said they'd started to think about those issues on *10-1*. "Obviously songs like *Read About It* and *Short Memory*, *Tin-Legs*, and so forth are pretty specific about those sorts of things." But Peter, the meaning of the song is *not* "specific", at least not to me.

Which means it's all up to me to work out what the hell this song means. That "Tin Legs" reference would surely have to be something to do with World War II fighter pilot Douglas Bader. He actually ended up with two tin legs after crashing his plane while training as a pilot for the First World War. One got chopped off immediately after the crash and doctors were forced to amputate the other one in hospital a short time thereafter. Despite the disability, when the Second World War came around, he cajoled the powers that be until they let him back in the cockpit. There was a biography written about him – called *Reach for the Sky*. They made a movie out of it too.

This song, which includes Bader's "Tin Legs" nickname in the title, also has the phrase "reach for the sky" at the start of the second verse. It's hard to see that as a coincidence. So I read his biography and watched the film but came away with nothing that seemed to link back to the song. No references to a Polish Disneyland, super computers or polar bear pride. Nor anything to do with wet dream control (yeah, the lyric sheet says the line is "we dream control", but there's no way Garrett sings "we"). I couldn't even find a reference to tin mines. What I did come away with was the impression that despite his perseverance and desire to overcome his disability, Bader seemed rather an insufferable person.

On the "Tin Mines" side of the song title, there were issues with tin mines in Tasmania in mid-1982 – when the band was recording the album. Renison Goldfields Consolidated announced plans to cut back on mining at its Renison tin mine and Mt Lyell copper mines. This wasn't good news for a state that was already experiencing its highest unemployment rate – 9.1 per cent – since the depression. The slowdown would include a four-day working week and two four-week shutdowns until the demand for tin and copper picked up. Perhaps this is the origin of the references in the second verse about crying in hope that there will be a tomorrow, that it's time to start working it out. Perhaps that's the workers wondering if they'll still have a job when the sun comes up tomorrow, all the while expecting someone else to fix the problem.

And the supercomputer being the new contraband? Maybe that's an oblique reference to technology and computerisation taking away manual jobs, like mining.

So my take on the song is that it's a lament for the jobs lost in a changing world and concern that no one seems to be doing anything to help (the "who's running the world" line). The apparent Bader references may be pointing to the need for those seeing a future that may take away their livelihood to persevere no matter what life throws at them.

But that talk of Disneyland, polar bears and Poland? Well, I have no clue what the band was on about there. And wet dream control? I don't even want to think about that one.

Somebody's Trying to Tell Me Something
(Hirst/Rotsey/Moginie/Gifford/Garrett)
3.58

The members of Midnight Oil have always been fiercely protective of their privacy. They're happy to stand up onstage in front of audiences around the world. Some of the members are happy to talk about the music and the band. But, if there is an imaginary line drawn in the Midnight Oil sand, it's right there. They'll perform, they'll talk about the songs they're performing but that's it. Pretty much everything else is off-limits.

They're not likely to talk about their private life; their partners, wives, ex-wives. Aside from Garrett, none of the other band members turn up to red-carpet events and get papped (or maybe they do but the paps only recognise the towering Garrett). They don't sell the rights for their wedding to magazines or newspapers. If there is any scandalous behaviour going on, they keep it all very, very quiet.

The "worst" thing (and it's not really even bad at all) I could find was that Hirst had fathered a child with a girlfriend back before Midnight Oil existed. The girlfriend was sent to Adelaide by her parents, the baby girl taken away as soon as she was born and fake names entered into her birth documents. The child was adopted by an Adelaide family and it wasn't until 2010 when musician Jay O'Shea's mother went looking for her that they were reunited. In an email mother sent to daughter was Hirst's name. The pair would meet up and eventually record together.

Yeah, I know, even their "scandals" have a happy ending.

When it comes to keeping things quiet, no band member does it better than the walking enigma that is Martin Rotsey. For a man who has been the lead guitarist of one of Australia's biggest bands for more than a quarter of a century to have a Wikipedia page that totals all of three paragraphs is unbelievable. This is all because he keeps his mouth shut, at least publicly. If somebody in the band is trying to tell you something, it sure as hell won't be Rotsey.

Of all the members past and present, only Rotsey

declined to chat on the record with Dodshon for his biography on the band. He only gave away a few quotes for Andrew McMillan's book *Strict Rules* and they appear to be things McMillan overheard rather than anything said directly to him in an interview (though he did admit that talking about himself made him "feel like a right wally"). Also, in the course of research for this book, I didn't uncover a single print interview in which quotes from Rotsey's mouth appear.

He is so very much the silent man that I was genuinely shocked when I heard him speak four whole words in their episode of the Music Max *Artist's Story* series. The four Australian-based band members were being interviewed as a group – Garrett and Hirst up front and Rotsey and Moginie behind them. I wondered why the hell they had Rotsey there given we surely wouldn't hear a peep out of him. Almost 15 minutes in, while they were answering a question about their *Countdown* non-appearance, Hirst looks over his right shoulder to Rotsey, who looks back and says "we didn't do it". That Rotsey opened his mouth in an interview seems to come as a shock to Hirst and Garrett, who both break out laughing.

The only other two instances I found of a Rotsey chat were a 20-second interview on a promo video for the 1993 *Earth and Sun and Moon* album and a short radio chat where he talks about supporting AC/DC back in the early days. I found those via the Facebook page of the Powderworkers, an ultra-hardcore group of fans. These super-fans go to see not only Oils shows, but those of various members' side projects, seem to each own a staggering amount of Oils shirts, posters and paraphenalia and will post on the page any image that even remotely looks like the band's hand logo. And even *they* express surprise when Rotsey speaks.

As far as the outside world is concerned, there might not be a whole lot of words passing Rotsey's lips. But within the inner sanctum of the band, his words carry a lot of weight. When it comes to songs and musical ideas, he's the bullshit detector. If the cool, silent Rotsey doesn't buy it, the band doesn't do it.

"Someone like Martin was so important in the band because if it didn't get past Martin it usually meant it wasn't any good," Moginie told the *Depth Perception* podcast.

"He would be the arbiter of good taste. He wouldn't be 'that sucks', he'd be 'well not that one but this one's really good'. So he'd have a good way of dealing with it. People would sometimes get really passionate about things and he would defuse all that. Without Martin I think it would have been a lot more difficult with the interband politics."

In terms of songwriting, *Somebody's Trying to Tell Me Something* was one of only a handful of times when the entire band was credited with a song. It's also the only song on the whole *10-1* album where Gifford got a credit – his first since the *Bird Noises* EP where the band was credited with every song. According to Dodshon, the all-band credit tends to mean the song was worked up from a jam rather than one or two members putting their heads together and bringing in a largely finished product to run through Rotsey's bullshit detector.

For Hirst, on at least two occasions he's pointed to this song as an example of the tension the band was under at the time. For Divola's *Rolling Stone* piece, he said "when Pete screams at the end of *Somebody's Trying to Tell Me Something*, that's a real scream. Everyone was feeling it, I think." And in the book *Your Name's on the Door* he tags this song and *Only The Strong* as "wild stuff".

"I think it's a great combination of a band at its angriest, at its poorest and at its most desperate, with a producer who could actually get those sounds on record and make it jump out of your speakers rather than be muffled somewhere in your woofer."

It's somewhat apt that this song sparks somewhat negative memories for Hirst, because the lyrics read like a diary of how the band felt during the make-or-break recording of the album. With references to cracking up, pressure being brought to bear, desperate voices and death by listening, you can easily read it as an lyrical outpouring of the tension and stresses weighing the band down as they try and come up with something that will allow the band to keep going. And be able to pay back the bank manager too.

Here are a few observations about the song. First, Garrett's lead vocal; the song clocks in a whisker under four minutes and yet any genuine lead vocals finish less than halfway through. After that, it's that scream and a whole lot of random noises from the big bald guy. Hard to think of too many songs – from any band at all – where the singer spout gibberish noises for half the song. And he only ever sings the title of the song once – *Somebody's Out There* would have been a better choice of title. Or maybe even *Breaking Me Down*, which is the first and last line we hear.

Then there's that impossibly fat bassline during the song's one chorus (yeah, technically it only has one chorus). How good is that? It's like they said "okay, Giffo, the floor is yours in the chorus, give us what you got". And he reels off that huge monster of a bassline. It's like it's played on bass strings the size of tow cables

What else is there? Oh yeah, that infinite groove at the end. I'm not sure if that's what it's called but it sounds cool so I'm going with it. That's the bit around 30 seconds from the end of the song where the final line of "breaking me down" simply keeps on going. Forever. Well, it does on my vinyl copy, because my record player is crap and the arm never lifts up at the end of an album. That wouldn't work on CD (or cassette, if you're old like me) so they had the vocal run for about 30 seconds before cutting out. I think that's the better version as listening to the endless groove for more than a minute really does your head in.

I know because I tried to see how long I could stand it. At about the 50-second mark that vocal starts to feel like a drill working its way through your ear canal.

Red Sails in the Sunset

Released October 1984

So here we are, at the best album in the Midnight Oil catalogue. A lot of people will disagree with that assessment. But those people are wrong and here's why. It's the band at their wildest, at their most adventurous, their most eccentric, where they've given free rein to their "what happens if we do this" urges. And yet the album never loses focus, the band never goes overboard or takes things too far. No, I don't consider the breathy Darth Vader effect in *Harrisburg* taking things too far, it adds a sense of vague malevolence to a song about a near nuclear meltdown in suburbia.

Red Sails in the Sunset has so many different levels and textures that expose themselves over time. Seriously, how can you not have anything but love and admiration for an album that has the likes of *Best of Both Worlds*, *Kosciusko*, *Jimmy Sharman's Boxers* and the overwhelming *Bells and Horns in the Back of Beyond?*

It was the band's first No1 album. It's true – while *10-1* stayed in the charts for a couple of years it never reached the top spot. It has the band's best album cover – in fact it's one of the best covers of any band anywhere (though what it represents is often misunderstood by people).

It contains the band's shortest song of any album in *Bakerman*. It would also pick up the daily double of having the longest song too – *Jimmy Sharman's Boxers* – were it not for *Nothing Lost - Nothing Gained* from their debut. Though there is some flab in the latter song's eight and a half minutes, while the 7.22 run time of *Boxers* contains not a wasted second.

It contains the only Midnight Oil song that features no members of Midnight Oil (I'm pretty sure that's right; the album credits back me up on that score). And also the first writing credit to a non-member.

It could even be argued that the band doesn't get to the far more popular *Diesel and Dust* without going through *Red Sails in the Sunset*. Midnight Oil's musical journey was mapped out just as much by deciding where they didn't want to go as where they did ("it's part of the psychology of the band that we would tend to swing away from what we'd done previously," Garrett said in the *Full Tank* liner notes).

And one way they worked out where they didn't want to go was to look over their shoulder. *In Red Sails*, they'd already taken the studio experimentation as far as they desired or dared, so whatever came immediately afterwards was going to be more stripped back, more basic and less fiddly. (they did the same with *Earth and Sun and Moon*, which was clearly a move away from the radio-friendly sheen of *Diesel* and *Blue Sky Mining*).

But despite all this *Red Sails* greatness, there are plenty of people don't have much admiration for this album. In the Midnight Oil catalogue, it seems to be the least liked. And that's including the band's last few albums, the ones that sales figures suggest were only bought by the hardcore fans.

To me part of the reason why this is so – and why *Red Sails* is treated like a red-headed stepchild – is because of where it sits in the catalogue. It's smack in between the band's two biggest albums – *10-1* and *Diesel and Dust*. There it is, like an overlooked middle child having to suffer under the endless attention fawned on the siblings on either side. I mean, there are at least two documentaries on the making of *10-1* and the lead-up to *Diesel and Dust* got its own book in the form of *Strict Rules*. But *Red Sails* – that deep, complicated, challenging record with a real story to tell? Well, that gets ignored.

Until now, I guess.

When it came time to record a follow-up to *10-1*, rather than head back to England for the third time, the band went to Tokyo. They went there for what would be three months – June, July and August – in the Orwellian year of 1984. The reasons they went over there are many and varied – Sony, their new label, wanted a western band to record in Japan; the band figured Japanese studios would have first-class recording equipment; they now had some money to play with; Martin Rotsey had lived there in his teens and spoke very highly of the place.

That last one comes from the mouth of Garrett, though McMillan says in *Strict Rules* that Rotsey was sent to Sydney Grammar as a boarder while his parents went to Japan. Rotsey's the guy who would know the truth, though he's unlikely to pipe up and tell us.

The idea was to take things a step further than *10-1*, to use the studio as another instrument. "We tried to do a little bit more of what we started to do with *10, 9,8*," Garrett told Bill Wolfe in *Spin* magazine, "which was marry sophisticated technological studio hardware with primitive sounds." Hirst told an Australian newspaper "…we wanted acoustic sounds everywhere rather than electric sounds. Plus we decided not to baulk at any musical decision. If the record needed a clarinet or a brass section or a school band we'd get one."

Years later, in his book *Willie's Bar and Grill*, Hirst would describe the recording process thus; "we threw so many sounds into the pot – a sumo wrestler's soup of samples, cheesy keyboards, gongs and a saki-soaked orchestra."

The band – with producer Launay in tow – rocked up at the Victor Studio in the Tokyo suburb of Aoyama. Also along for the ride, says Hirst, was a translator named Mr Shapiro (reportedly an American sumo wrestler) who was able to explain to engineers Shigio and Yoshi just what hand signals Launay would use for "stop", "record" and "erase".

One thing they forgot to bring was songs; unlike *10-1*, where all the songs were written and well-rehearsed before entering the studio, the band were winging it a bit in Tokyo.

"We had a pretty heavy touring schedule and something in the band had changed," Moginie told Depth Perception. "It became more about doing gigs. So by the time we came to do *Red Sails* we didn't have a lot of songs up our sleeves."

The few songs they did have were recorded quickly. "Then there was another period that we went into where we didn't quite have the songs so we used a drum machine to do the song on and then we'd play to that," Moginie said. "And that didn't sound quite right so we'd muck around with that."

The message here is, to Moginie's ears, *Red Sails* isn't the band at their finest moment. While saying he doesn't want to put it down because some people really like it, he found it "a slightly unfocused, sprawling opus".

To Garrett's ears, the resulting album was very Australian. "*Red Sails*, for one reason or another," he told *LA Times* journalist Duncan Strauss, "became a particularly Australian album. We were talking last night about maybe putting a glossary of terms in with the record, so people could find their way through it."

It's a sentiment Hirst echoed to *Spin*'s Wolfe. "Typical Oils, really: on the verge of international success and we make a record that only third-generation antipodeans can understand."

There's no doubt *Red Sails in the Sunset* is the outlier in the Oils canon. It is undeniably odd, which would seem to be a byproduct of both the desire to experiment in the studio and also the eye-opening experience of a different culture. "We wanted to absorb a myriad of influences to push us somewhere else," Hirst told MusicMax's Chit Chat. "so Japan was all over the album."

In Dodshon's bio, Launay said the band went a bit

kooky; "Everyone was wearing colourful clothes, bright colours. We all ended up wearing pink and green sneakers." He also found the engineers Shigio and Yoshi had a very different way of working; after a month Launay found the two were taking all the microphones down and packing them away each night, only to pull them out and set them up again each morning – with the help of Polaroid photos taken the night before.

As was the case with *10-1*, there seems to be a real possibility at the time that *Red Sails in the Sunset* could end up being the band's last hurrah. Not because of the "make or break" pressure the band put on themselves (as was the case with *10-1*) but rather Garrett's political ambitions. Before leaving for Tokyo, he'd been involved in starting up Nuclear Disarmament Projects "to raise the alarm about the nuclear madness we feared was infecting the world".

During the *Red Sails* sessions Garrett knew he might be tapped on the shoulder by the Nuclear Disarmament Party (NDP) to run as a candidate for the Senate in NSW. That obviously would be a distraction for the singer – in his autobiography he said "my mind wasn't fixed on songs and recording", adding that he had little to bring to the table in Tokyo.

It wasn't until the band's return to Australia that

Garrett told them of his intention to run for the Senate. While Garrett has said he didn't feel it would be the end of the band if he became a politician (though he changed his mind when he looked to become a Labor MP) two other members didn't agree. Hirst felt squeezing in rehearsals, recording sessions and tours in between Senate sittings wasn't going work long-term. Bassplayer Gifford saw Garrett's election as saying goodbye to Midnight Oil as they knew it. Hirst has since backtracked (as in the *Midnight Oil: 1984* documentary) and stated he never felt the band would cease if Garrett got elected. But his earlier statements would seem to be correct; politicians have a lot of demands on their time; and it's impossible to fathom the young, idealistic Garrett of the mid-1980s would sell short those who voted for him. So he'd definitely be a busy politician.

Doing all that during the day and then adding on top the role of a singer in a band at what was then the highest point in their career just seems impossible. For instance, that tour through Central Australia that informed the mega-selling *Diesel and Dust*? That probably doesn't happen if Garrett becomes a senator – where would he find the time to go bush for several weeks?

To my eyes, Senator Garrett would have meant

the decline of Midnight Oil, would have meant *Red Sails in the Sunset* was the band's swansong. Yet, to the band's credit they were happy to let him take the shot and run for office. They'd just climbed to the top of the mountain, become the biggest band in the country and they were willing to risk all that so Garrett could take a tilt at Canberra. That's an admirable sacrifice to make for your bandmate.

When *Red Sails in the Sunset* was released in October 1984, it went to No1 on the charts. In the US the record company reception resembled the one A&M gave *Place Without a Postcard*. They couldn't hear any hit singles and so delayed the release a few months while they tried to convince the band to go back and record some catchy tunes. "And of course, we said, 'Look, the album's the album'," Garrett told the *LA Times*.

The album title reaches back to an earlier release – *Wedding Cake Island* from the *Bird Noises* EP. Released as an instrumental, the surf tune initially sported a rant about real estate agents from Garrett over the top in which he yelled "red sails in the fucking sunset!".

"The reason it didn't make it onto the record," Garrett told *Roadrunner*'s Donald Robertson, "is because it's grossly libelous. Like it was just this monologue describing the trip up the coast, like a folklore kind of thing, but I got caught up on how Port Macquarie had been fucked up by developers. I named people.

"Real estate agents are one of my pet hates. I gave 'em a real hammering. Right over one of the nice guitar bits. I'm going 'aw fucking bullshit' blah, blah, blah — I got a bit excited."

Excited. That's how I'd describe my approach to *Red Sails in the Sunset*. But that's perhaps not the way Mr Willis at the Chatswood ANZ would feel. According to Hirst, the band's time in Tokyo left them owing the bank $1 million. To my ears, it was a price well worth paying.

Side One

When The Generals Talk
(Hirst/Moginie/Garrett)
3.31

Remember *Outside World*, the first song on *10,9,8*? Remember how it was so different from what fans had heard from the band up that point and how it would mess with their heads? I reckon the band went and did it again with the opening track on *Red Sails in the Sunset*.

They could have opened with *Best of Both Worlds*, which is definitely in the "ahh, yes this is what Midnight Oil is supposed to sound like" category. Sure, there is some brass there at the start of *Both Worlds*, but it's buried underneath that killer guitar riff from Rotsey and some frenetic drumming from Hirst.

In the end, that song sits in the second spot in the running order, so it wouldn't have been too much hassle to push it into the top spot.

But the first song was a rather un-Oils tune – *When the Generals Talk* – in which the first thing the listener hears is some electronic drums. My how things change; a few years ago, Hirst loathed the things, now he's gone and used them for the basis of a song (and in such a way that it would require the help of a roadie to play some of the beats live). Then, after the trio of electronic drum blasts, the listener hears a short proto-techno dance groove (how has no one since used this bit as a sample?). Jumping in next is stuttering '80s pop guitar riff and then what sounds very much like Garrett screaming.

At this stage the listener may well have asked 'What are the Oils doing? It's like they've gone all 'top 40'." And maybe they're a bit weirded out by a tune that sounds like a left turn for Midnight Oil, even given the change of direction taken by *10,9,8*.

But the big shock for that listener is just about to drop. The lyrics kick in on the tail of that Garrett scream. And what's this? That's not Garrett's voice singing. Remember, this was the first time someone who wasn't a 75ft tall bald guy sang lead on a Midnight Oil song.

And so the listener would race to the album cover and pull out that inner sleeve (assuming they don't already have it in their hands to look at while listening to a new album – it's what I always did when listening to something for the first time). They scan the cover and the inner sleeve for an explanation of just who that is singing the lead on the first track of this new album.

But there's nothing there – indeed the only member who gets a credit for what they did is Gary Morris, who has "business" listed next to his name. The listener would then take a stab, knowing Hirst and Gifford were the main backing vocalists, and figure that had to be the drummer singing. After all he's one of the credited songwriters.

Perhaps that sent a small shudder through the listener. For by the time *Red Sails in the Sunset* came out, Garrett had announced he was running for a seat in the federal Senate. Had Hirst decided now was the time to try his hand at lead vocals because Garrett was planning on leaving the band if he won the election? Was the band looking to set up a Plan B? Could we really expect to see Hirst singing lead on all the band's songs after the election? It may seem a bit silly now but at the time, there were questions being asked within the band as to what Garrett's election would mean, so it only makes sense that the fans would be wondering too. And opting to open the new album with a lead vocal from someone other than Garrett probably didn't really help calm the waters.

The Hirst lead vocal didn't come about because of the need for the band to plan for all possible futures. Garrett simply didn't like the song, at least not enough to want to sing it for himself. In an October 1984 interview with Mal Reding, Garrett – in a tone that seems somewhat disparaging – referred to *When the Generals Talk* as "a pop song".

"Rob Hirst might write a pop song," Garrett said. "Well, he has, in fact he wrote *Generals Talk* on the *Red Sails* album, which I just didn't feel comfortable singing a line like that. I'm happy for him to sing it."

Now, does that seem like Garrett was being at least a little bit dismissive of this song? I think so, especially when you consider Garrett's penchant for changing other people's lyrics to something he does feel comfortable singing. So it leaves me with the feeling what Garrett didn't like was the "pop" nature of the song itself and not the content of the lyrics.

Whatever the reason, it worked out for the best. Listening to the song now, it's hard to imagine Garrett doing a decent job of it. *When the Generals Talk* really is a *pop* song and I don't think Garrett's vocal stylings would work at all well here; they'd likely come off too harsh. What this pop song needed was the more melodic pop vocals of Hirst.

The track is almost a Hirst solo effort; as well as the vocals it's his drums that dominate the track. On each of the verses it's just Hirst there with his drums and voice. While that juddering guitar riff from Rotsey does capture the ear, this is really Hirst's baby (with some help from the other half of the rhythm section via a great climbing bass run from Gifford in the choruses – which is basically the only thing he's required to do in the whole song).

It's very different from anything the band has done before – or since, really. It even stands out from the other songs on the *Red Sails* album itself. Though, you could also say that about a few other tracks on this wonderfully eclectic, adventurous and odd release. Turns out it could have been even odder. Producer Launay told biographer Dodshon there was a plan to get a group of Japanese girls in to sing the chorus, though in the end they stuck with the harmonies of Hirst and Gifford – who are apparently trying to sing in the register of those girls.

To me this is an example of what I like to think of as the "controlled weirdness" in operation on *Red Sails in the Sunset*. Some people – including band members – feel they went off the rails with this release, but decisions like nixing the Japanese girls suggests there was still a semblance of control here; yes, they were going to experiment and try to stretch themselves, but they weren't going to go completely stupid. They walked the fine line between experimentation and indulgence, always managing to stay on the right side of it.

A final footnote: a cover of this song appears on the patchy tribute album *The Power & The Passion*. Released in 2001, it features Australian and New Zealand bands who were popular at the time (well, except for Waylayd – never heard of those guys). Some of the covers work, such as Bodyjar's blistering *Back on the Borderline*, the Regurgitator version of *Stand in Line* (which sounds like a tune from an '80s computer game) and David McCormack making *Power & the Passion* sound like one of *his* songs.

Other songs less so, such as the weird whispered vocals on The Superjesus' version of *Short Memory*, or Area 7's misguided effort to turn *Read About It* into a ska tune. Also in the latter camp is Jebediah's reworking of *When the Generals Talk*, which puts the guitars in the centre of the song rather than the drums. Given the drum and bass groove of the original, an electronic music exponent would have been a better option – they could have really done something with this tune.

Best of Both Worlds
(Hirst/Moginie)
4.03

This was the song that introduced me to Midnight Oil in late January 1985, while I was a few thousand feet in the air. My father had gotten a posting to the Australian embassy in Washington DC, so the whole family lived there for two and half years in the early 1980s. Which means I completely missed the breakthrough of *10-1*; while my friends in Australia were cranking out the Oils at home, I wasn't hearing a thing.

That changed in January 1985 when we boarded a Qantas plane and headed home. Back then the choice of in-flight entertainment was limited to a movie or one of a range of music channels that would cycle through the same 20-odd songs throughout the flight. Headphones on my ears, I flicked to the rock channel.

Near the top of the playlist was this song by a band I'd never heard of called Midnight Oil. That looping guitar riff kicked off the song and, when it finished four minutes later, I was hooked. I'd wait for the playlist to cycle through so I could hear that song again. And again. And again. And again. By the time the wheels of our plane touched the tarmac in Sydney I knew I'd have to find out some more about Midnight Oil. I thought that might be a little difficult, not aware this band I'd never heard of was the biggest in the country.

What I learned over time was that this band had an image of being, well, a bunch of complainers. All their songs seemed to be going on about something they thought was wrong in society. Hell, for all I knew, *Bakerman* was about some issue songwriter Hirst had with the guy who made his bread. Of course, the band wasn't a pack of whingers, really. Whingers just complain about the way things are without giving any thought to taking action and changing the status quo. Midnight Oil have made it a practice of putting their money where their mouth is. And often quite literally, when it comes to the countless benefit gigs the band has played.

But the image of the band as being perpetually serious, about playing "complaint rock" is one that always dogged the band (though, as Hirst wrote in

Willie's Bar and Grill, "it's better to play complaint rock than compliant rock"). That was a particular frustration of Moginie, the uber music geek in the band. For much of the band, Moginie was the shy awkward guy, who seemed like he'd much rather be at home than on the stage. But, eventually, he grew comfortable in his own skin and voiced his irritation with the public's focus on the subject matter of the songs, rather than the songs themselves.

While talking with Kruger for *Songwriters Speak*, Moginie used the example of the song *Surf's Up Tonight*, from the *Breathe* album – which was simply about having a surf.

"And of course the reviews were 'Oh, they're going on about water pollution'," he said. "So the image of the band took over and came back to bite us a little bit. You just couldn't write a song about something whimsical. It was always 'Oh, you're talking about something important. You must be. It's Midnight Oil'."

In a way, that issue has plagued *Best of Both Worlds* too. With lines about times being tough and things being rough, it's often been assumed the title of the song is ironic – that it's a jibe about the state of affairs in Australia.

But it's not. It's actually a positive song. Yep, a

positive song. From Midnight Oil. Hirst, one of the songwriters, said the inspiration came from the band's overseas travel.

"The song *Best of Both Worlds* is about being in Sydney," Hirst told *Spin* magazine's Wolf, "it's about what we have. We went back and there were more strikes on and the NSW government was exploding with corruption, but it seemed that – despite all these things – what was going on overseas was far, far worse, and we should just get our act together and realise what we've got."

Incidentally, Garrett feels the same way about another misunderstood song – *Lucky Country* from *Place Without a Postcard*. "This is the lucky country, he said to *Roadrunner*, "there's no question about that. People don't realise it, that's the problem. We feel strongly about it."

The song mightn't be about the country going down the toilet, but that's where Hirst was during the recording. The take of the drums we hear on *Best of Both Worlds* was recorded in the toilets of level three of the JVC Victor Studios in Tokyo. Hirst and his kit were set up there next to the urinals to take advantage of the acoustics. It must have been a strange site to those using the facilities – the toilet was still open for business while Hirst whacked away at his kit. Some studio employees scratched their heads at the strange ideas of these Australians, while at least one – studio boss Isamu Hachiguchi – voiced his displeasure.

"I'm interrupted by studio manager Hachiguchi-san, who bursts into the bathroom desperately waving his hands, signalling for me to cease and desist," Hirst said in a track-by-track look at the *Flat Chat* compilation CD.

"But I can't just stop – after all, we're in the middle of *the* take. So I plough on, risking a serious diplomatic rift in Australian/Japanese relations. When the song is secured, I'm soberly informed that an elderly national treasure and his wife were attempting to capture pristine recordings of koto and shamisen in the studio downstairs, when my kit noise came thundering down the stairwell."

The other oft-told story about the recording of this song is the one about the brass section being just too good. The band brought in a trumpet, trombone and saxophone player and they played a score written by Moginie – and it sounded terrible. Not on its own but in relation to the song; they sounded perfect, the band was looser. Moginie asked for it to be rawer and, after some to-ing and froing due to the language barrier, the brass trio finally got it – "more rock and roll!"

"So we ran the tape again and this time it was perfect – out of tune and out of time," Launay told biographer Dodshon.

The result is a little over four minutes of perfection – one of the best songs the band has written. I first heard it more than 30 years ago and I still haven't tired of it. It starts with that corkscrewing guitar riff from Moginie accompanied by Hirst's wild drumming, which sounds like he's playing while his kit is falling down a flight of stairs (managing to keep time as it falls too). And we get our first taste of that Japanese "rock and roll!" brass section. After 25 seconds of that rollicking intro, we get to Garrett's vocal (which is either double-tracked or features Hirst and Gifford harmonising almost all the way through) which appears to start with what could be best described as the chorus.

His punchy vocal delivery accentuates the stabbing guitar riffs going on behind him. Then the intro resurfaces, before we go into the "is it the chorus" for a second time. Then we get what could be a verse, which slows things down a bit so we can catch our breath before the brass comes in to amp things up again, bringing us to Rotsey riff where it sounds like he's trying to strangle his guitar (or maybe squeeze out every single note).

And it's the verse again, which rises to the end via some vaguely unnerving shouted vocals from Garrett. Then cue Rotsey with another frenetic solo before we head into the chorus again, wondering if we can get another break from the intensity of the song. Nope, because from here they rock out all the way through to the end.

While the song it an absolute ripper, the same can't really be said about the video. It really is a patchy effort; the sped-up and slowed-down live footage works a treat – and could have carried the video on its own. What lets things down is the glaringly cheap sci-fi special effects as a backdrop, and those really odd "floating sausages" at the end. While acknowledging the cheap effects, Garrett said on Music Max's *Kings of the Mountain* special it was still "worth watching".

"It's a strong song of course but you've got to have a chuckle when you're trying to create a science fiction film clip with a budget that enables you to do about 15 seconds of shooting a milk bar," he said.

"The best part of course is where the sausages get lowered down on fishing line and we try and puncture the sausages. This was our way of making movies. I hope people laugh at least."

It may be the case that Hirst wasn't a fan of the sci-fi effects and choose to avoid the studio session.

While he's seen frequently in the live footage portions of the video, he doesn't seem to appear in the studio footage in front of aluminium foil asteroids, cheap rockets and sausages on fishing line. There are a few quick cutaways taken from behind the kit where the drummer raises his arm in time with the music, but his face is turned away from the camera.

Once you notice this it truly appears as though Hirst didn't turn up to the shoot (for whatever reason) and the video maker is getting around it by using a stand-in – hence the only shots of the drummer are those that don't show his face. He's also the only member absent during the sausage spearing at the end – though if you watch closely Moginie is always on the edges of the frame, as though he's trying to stay out of shot as well.

If that's true then I can't blame them. That sausage scene wasn't one of Midnight Oil's best moments.

Sleep
(Moginie/Hirst/Garrett)
5.08

Oils on the Water, the concert film from the Goat Island show is a great video document of the *Red Sails in the Sunset* period. Of the 16 songs the band played on that Saturday afternoon/evening in January 1985, seven of them come from the album released just three months earlier. That means we're seeing the band running through the songs while they're still fresh, while they're still excited to be playing new material.

The material is so new, in fact, that the band stuffs things up on a few tunes, including Rotsey muffing the guitar riff coming out of the "fat cats" bit in *When the Generals Talk* (much to the evident amusement of Garrett and Gifford) and Garrett forgets to come in right at the start of *Minutes to Midnight*.

The show boasts a relaxed vibe, with the band really enjoying themselves. Which is to be expected when you consider the timing. Just weeks earlier Garrett found out he'd lost his tilt at the Senate. Aside from a warm-up up gig on the northern NSW coast a few days earlier, this is the first show since that news dropped. So we're watching a band dealing with the relief that they still *are* a band, that things won't have to change – or even perhaps end. Garrett himself looks really happy, as though he's reveling in the fact he doesn't have to give up standing at the front of this beast known as Midnight Oil. Next time you watch the DVD, just pay attention to how many times he smiles – the guy is absolutely loving it.

Moginie felt the same way, writing a letter in the bonus content of the *Best of Both Worlds* double concert DVD, "watching Goat Island I see a band at full tilt. Peter letting off steam after the campaign, cutting loose, joyous and proud even though he wasn't a Canberra suit."

Garrett and the rest of the band mightn't have been so chuffed if manager Gary Morris' initial idea for the gig venue got up. Writing in *RAM*, Andrew McMillan said the event started out as a private party at the Triple J Forbes Street, Sydney, HQ. The band would play on the roof and the gig would be beamed to the partygoers below in the studio via closed circuit TV.

Morris didn't like the idea and started thinking bigger – much bigger. "Why not stage the party (and the band) on the deck of the decommissioned aircraft carrier HMAS Melbourne?" McMillan paraphrased Morris in the *RAM* story. "A massive grey hulk that's moored off Bradley's Head. Awaiting its sale to the Japanese or Korean scrap metal merchants and its ultimate conversion into razor blades and Datsuns".

Midnight Oil playing on a warship? Surely, not.

"Triple J staff were aghast," McMillan wrote, "and reminded him that perhaps the band with their anti-nuke stance wouldn't like to perform on a military ship."

Eyes then turned to Sydney Harbour. Fort Denison was considered for the gig but deemed too small. Enter Goat Island, known to the locals before the arrival of the Europeans as Me-Mel and the birthplace of Bennelong (the first Aboriginal man to establish any sort of lasting relationship with the white newcomers).

Since 1788, the island just 500 metres from the mainland has been used as a quarry, an arsenal, a base for the Water Police and a bacteriology station during an outbreak of the bubonic plague in 1900. In the 1940s, the construction of wharves and shipyard facilities began and the 1950s saw the island become a popular site for dances; by that time the families of workers were living on the island.

But for one weekend in mid-January 1985, Midnight Oil owned the place. The gig had grown beyond being just a party for Triple J workers and became a listener competition. To enter all people had to do was write down the names of their top three bands and send them in (hence the "diligent supporters of the post office" reference from Garrett in the intro to *Minutes to Midnight*). "We can't tell you what the prize is," they told listeners, "but we know you're going to like it."

The first 75 entries that had Midnight Oil in the top spot were told "bring a friend and meet us down at the Harbour Master's steps at Circular Quay, at 6.30pm on Sunday, January 13. We're going for a ride".

Anyone not lucky enough to win had to wait until the following Saturday, when government broadcaster ABC aired the concert footage, simulcast on Triple J.

"To celebrate 10 years as the leading exponent of local and international new music," read a newspaper ad, "JJJ presents Midnight Oil in concert, simulcast from Goat Island. Switch your television to the ABC and your local ABC FM radio station up as loud as you can at 10.25 this Saturday night. Then just sit back and enjoy the power and the passion of the most talked about group in Australia."

One interesting point was raised by *Sydney Morning Herald* journalist Ed St John in a preview of the TV broadcast; despite it being a JJJ party, there was nothing onstage to suggest that. "Unlike previous 2JJJ/Midnight Oil concerts, no station logos were visible on the concert stage, suggesting that the band regards the concert footage, to which it has access outside Australia, as an ideal promotional tool in the international market."

I'm not sure if that was the band's intention, but you have to admit that concert footage with the Sydney Harbour as a backdrop is a pretty effective promotional tool. It's certainly a beautiful concert to watch - especially as the sun sets during *Tin-Legs & Tin Mines* and the city lights come on. If your band only had one concert DVD to put forward to the world, then Goat Island is a pretty good one. Though, given it's heavy with *Red Sails in the Sunset* tunes, I could easily be a bit biased.

Sleep is one of the seven songs from the *Red Sails* album performed at Goat Island and, until I started the research for this book, I had the wrong idea what the song was about. My guess was way off – I thought it had something to do with walking home after a big night out where things didn't go the way you planned. Must have been that stuff about shoe leather being worn out.

But according to a Bill Wolfe piece in *Spin* magazine, the song "describes Aborigines who venture into the cities and end up as unemployed alcoholics, often spending brutal nights in jail." That makes more sense, and better explains the references to Missionbeat (a service that patrols Sydney streets aiming to offer help for the homeless), being stuck in a cell and looking for sleep to take you away from all that.

Minutes to Midnight
(Moginie/Garrett)
3.07

"As we enter the new year, hope is eclipsed by foreboding. The accelerating nuclear arms race and the almost complete breakdown of communication between the superpowers have combined to create a situation of extreme and immediate danger.

"In response to these trends and as a warning of where they lead, we have moved the Bulletin's doomsday clock forward by one minute – to three minutes before midnight. It is a measure of the gravity of the current situation that only once in our 39-year history – in 1953 in response to the advent of the hydrogen bomb – have we seen fit to place the warning hand any closer to midnight than it stands today."

So said the editorial from the January 1984 edition of the *Bulletin of the Atomic Scientists*, explaining why that clock on the wall now read three minutes until midnight. Created by artist Martyl Langsdorf for the *Bulletin*, the clock surfaced in 1947 as a metaphor for explaining how close humanity was to blowing up the world. A clock was chosen because it was a reflection of the sense of urgency that had to be conveyed.

In 1947 it was set up to read seven minutes to midnight, because Langsdorf felt "it looked good to my eyes". Since then the decision to move the hands of the clock is treated more seriously – that decision is made by the *Bulletin*'s Science and Security Board after discussing the issue and seeking input from Nobel laureates and others.

As of 2018, the closest the hands have been to signalling Armageddon was two minutes to midnight – in 1953 and again in 2018. The furthest apart they've been was in 1991 with the US and Soviet Union signing the Strategic Arms Reduction Treaty which wound the clock all the way to 17 minutes to midnight.

The action in January 1984 to bring the hands to three minutes to midnight – the closest to midnight they'd been in more than 30 years – was taken just months before the band would head to Tokyo to record the *Red Sails in the Sunset*. And would very much inform the song *Minutes to Midnight*, with its references to military hardware. That includes AWACS, which stands for Airborne Warning and Control System, and refers to a surveillance aircraft with a big radar attached to its back designed to detect movement of enemy aircraft, ships and other vehicles.

There are also references to missiles, such as America's ICBM (Intercontinental Ballistic Missile) and the Russian SS-20 – the latter were designed to be carried and shot off the back of a large truck, which made them mobile and harder for an enemy to deal with than a missile in a silo. And the fingers blistering on the 88s, I presume that's a reference to an anti-tank gun the Nazis used during World War II.

There also seems to be a nuclear reference to science fiction author HG Wells in the song. A far back as 1913 he imagined the use of atomic weapons, in a novel he wrote called *The World Set Free*. However, these atomic bombs are far different than the one we saw in action in Hiroshima.

Wells' atomic bombs have no more force than other high explosives and are treated more like a hand grenade than a bomb dropped from the bowels of an aircraft. Here's how Wells described the process of using the bomb.

"The gaunt face hardened to grimness, and with

both hands the bombthrower lifted the big atomic bomb from the box and steadied it against the side. It was a black sphere two feet in diameter. Between its handles was a little celluloid stud, and to this he bent his head until his lips touched it. Then he had to bite in order to let the air in upon the inductive. Sure of its accessibility, he craned his neck over the side of the aeroplane and judged his pace and distance. Then very quickly he bent forward, bit the stud, and hoisted the bomb over the side."

As to what the racehorse Phar Lap in a jar of liquid has to do with nuclear war, your guess is as good as mine.

The Bulletin of Atomic Scientists wasn't overreacting when it moved the hands of the clock; the early 1980s wasn't a great time for those wishing to avoid dying in a massive explosion of radiation. Ronald Reagan was in the White House and, despite claiming to want to rid the world of nuclear weapons, really gave the USSR – and the rest of the world – every indication that he was itching to push the big red button.

In the early 1980s the USSR was governed by a series of ageing leaders who started dropping like flies; Leonid Brezhnev died in 1982, his successor Yuri Andropov two years later, and *his* successor

Konstantin Chernenko lasted just 11 months in the job before he died and was replaced by Mikhail Gorbachev.

They'd been chosen from the increasingly paranoid (and stupid) governing body the Politburo, which was full of men who'd grown up in the Cold War era and were very, very suspicious of the United States. So much so the KGB created Operation RyaN, to try and detect preparations for a US nuclear strike. The measures it asked its US agents to look for were often ridiculous; counting the number of lights on in buildings like the Ministry of Defence because officials working late could be seen as last-minute preparation for war. Seems they didn't consider it would more likely be a sign of cleaners going about their work in the early hours.

What the US military did to the Russians in the early 1980s was exactly what you don't do with paranoid people – give them a reason to think they're right to be paranoid. During the early 1980s the US military would goad the Soviets, just to see how far they could be pushed and how they would react.

In September 1982, two US aircraft carriers – the USS Enterprise and USS Midway – intentionally came within a few hundred kilometres of the Soviets' major Pacific naval base. Then the ships sailed south along the Kuril Islands – which were Russian property. It was an action as provocative as the Soviets turning up off the shore of Alaska.

A few months later, the Enterprise happened upon a Soviet aircraft carrier and decided to launch "a practice long-range strike" against it. The captain unleashed a number of jet fighters, had them engage visual contact with the carrier and then turn around.

In April, US ships carried out an exercise in the Pacific, sending jets in the air around the clock with the explicit aim of getting the Soviets to switch on their radar and scramble fighters ready to respond to the apparent threat. During the exercise, the Midway switched off all electronic equipment and headed to the Kurils. Fighter planes from the Midway violated Soviet airspace, which caught their air force by surprise. The ongoing antics of the US military had put the Russians on edge and they vowed to take action should they invade Soviet airspace again.

These US-USSR tensions would have very grave consequences for passengers on board a Korean airliner. On August 31, 1983, Korean Air Lines flight 007 took off from Anchorage, Alaska, headed to Seoul, South Korea. For reasons that are still not known, the plane gradually drifted off course headed towards the Kamchatka Peninsula of the Soviet

Union. Also in the air that night was a US air force spy plane – a converted Boeing 707 passenger plane. As the spy plane circled overhead, waiting to record a rumoured Soviet missile test, KAL 007 was to its south.

And here is the critical moment. The Soviets had been tracking the spy plane on radar but did not see it turn and head back to base. It crossed the flight path of 007, and the Soviets then tracked that passenger plane all the while thinking it was the spying aircraft it had noticed earlier.

As the radar operators watched, the plane kept on its heading that would take it over Soviet airspace. Soon fighters were sent up to engage with what they thought was the spy plane (in a tragic coincidence, a both the spy plane and a 747 looked quite similar). The lead pilot tried to contact the civilian airliner, but to no avail. He was ordered to flash his own lights as a warning, followed by a cannon burst across its flight path. But there was no response.

With the recent US air incursions still at the forefront of their minds, the commanders on the ground gave the order to open fire. At 3.25am, the pilot launched two missiles, one of them a heat-seeker. Thirty seconds later it found the target and 269 people lost their lives. US President Ronald Reagan was outraged, labelling it "an act of barbarism, born of a society which wantonly disregards individual rights and the value of human life". The Soviets didn't help the situation by taking days to even acknowledge the shooting down of the aircraft.

The reality was that the shooting down of KAL 007 was a tragic accident. And one in which the seeds were sown by the aggressive actions of the US military over the previous 12 months.

What the Americans did next would unknowingly bring the world within a whisker of nuclear war. On November 20, US TV aired the movie *The Day After*, about the start of a nuclear war. The show horrified and scared the nation but few realised they had come close to the real thing just a few weeks earlier.

In the first week of November, NATO started a military exercise called Able Archer 83. It would be a full-scale simulation of the firing of nuclear weapons in a European conflict. The Russians were always wary that a military exercise could be used as a cover for a genuine first strike, because that was one of the tactics in their own playbook. So they were on edge for Able Archer.

That tension increased when the NATO procedures started to differ from what the Soviets had noted in previous exercises. When, six days into Able

Archer, they noticed the NATO top secret codes had changed, the USSR was convinced a first strike was coming.

So Premier Andropov ordered his country's nuclear arsenal be put on the maximum state of alertness. Officers in missile silos were shadowed by KGB agents to ensure they would act on any order to fire should it be delivered. Jet fighters were fully armed and fueled, pilots instructed to wait at the end of the runway with the engine running ready for take-off.

But the Soviet leaders never issued the launch codes, never ordered the planes to take off. And the NATO allies completed Able Archer 83, totally unaware of what they had provoked in the USSR.

It's in this world climate that gave rise to the fear of nuclear annihilation around the world, a fear reflected on *Red Sails in the Sunset*.

Something else that is noticeable on *Minutes to Midnight* is what Gifford referred to in an online interview as "god bothering". "I noticed a change in Peter Garrett when he started running for politics," Gifford wrote. "He was (rightly) being more careful in what he said publicly and there was a bit of God bothering on *Red Sails*."

In a profile on Garrett, journalist and friend David Leser states the opinions of friends that the singer suffered a "spiritual crisis" at the time of *Red Sails* and turned to Christianity (it also had Garrett stating he's opposed to abortion, IVF and, it appears from the context, euthanasia. "If you're going to place certain values on life, somewhere you have to draw the line," he explained).

In the piece Hirst offers support for that claim; "Pete became a Christian in that year and became a very different person in subsequent months. Most people who become Christian, or have some spiritual revelation, go through a very tortured period and he did, I believe, as well."

Garrett admitted in his autobiography *Big Blue Sky* that he read "*Gideon's Bible* and the sayings of Buddha" while in Tokyo in 1984, because they were the only English language books in his hotel. In Leser's piece, Garrett said he "re-embraced" his faith during those months in Tokyo in 1984. "It was a turning point in terms of becoming invigorated," Garrett said. "Well … I think you've got to get down on your knees and I think you've got to say 'I'm stuffing up'."

Any so-called "god bothering" is most evident on *Minutes to Midnight*, including the opening line about God being good – a phrase that is repeated a number of times throughout the song. There's also a possible Biblical link to the "talking in tongues" line. The reference to ears not hearing and eyes not seeing, well that's strikingly similar to a passage in Jeremiah 5:21 which reads "Hear this, you foolish and senseless people, who have eyes but do not see, who have ears but do not hear".

At the end of the day, the religious beliefs of the band's lead singer don't really seem to matter too much. Well, they obviously matter a great deal to *him*, but they don't affect the enjoyment of the band's output in any way. It's only noticeable in this song because of the explicit use of the word "God". Without that one word, the other Biblical references would have been missed by most people, leaving us to conclude this is just a song about nuclear war, when it seems to also be about faith in the face of a threat.

Jimmy Sharman's Boxers
(Hirst/Moginie)
7.22

There were actually two Jimmy Sharmans, a father and his son. While they would both become known for travelling boxing tents – where the public could enter the ring and punch on with a real boxer – the family didn't invent them. The boxing tent concept had been around since the late 1800s.

Sharman senior fought in the tents in the early 20th century before deciding to give up fighting and run his own tent instead. The reason for that varies – Sharman was a showman who would rework a story to suit the audience. One version has him so horrified at the injuries he meted out to boxer Jack Carter in 1912 that he gave up fighting and chose to become a promoter. Another version has it that an exploding ammonia bottle damaged his sight and forced him to give up the game.

According to Peter Corris' history of boxing in Australia, Sharman started out at the country town of Temora and then "inspired presumably by the tent shows he had known as a youth, Sharman decided to take it to the road". While he was in competition with other troupes, he eventually came to dominate the scene to the extent that when people thought of tent boxing, they thought of Sharman.

At rural shows around the country and in capital cities too he used a bass drum to get the public's attention and to call for challengers (hence the "roll up, roll up" intro to the song and the use of a marching bass drum as seen in the Goat Island concert).

Garrett told journalist Mal Reding that songwriter Hirst had seen some of those touring Sharman shows.

"He remembers going out to see, as many young Australians would, circuses or fairs that we had in the '50s and '60s," Garrett said.

"One of the attractions was called the Jimmy Sharman Boxing Tent. It was a tent with a boxing ring inside and you paid to go and see members of the public fight against the boxing troupe, which was for the most part made up of Aboriginals.

"In the early days the Aboriginal boxers were very badly paid and quite often they would be ill-matched against larger, heftier Australian versions, who perhaps they could box better than. To equalise the fight and make it more exciting for the people they would be mismatched."

That's something backed up by Corris' history, where it's suggested race and colour were factors in Sharman's line-up of boxers. "Rud Kee, a capable fighter, inspired many challenges from men who thought themselves naturally superior to a Chinese. No Sharman line-up failed to include Aborigines whose appearances, especially in the country towns, added spice to the performances."

Hirst's own memories of seeing the Sharman tent were not pleasant. "My earliest remembrance of Sharman's tents is a depressing scene with the big drum he used to beat madly resounding through the whole show, and 12 or 13 Aboriginal boxers looking like the most tragic, pathetic human beings you've ever seen standing up there in various states of disarray, he told *Spin* magazine.

Around this time, Sharman Jr took over the running of the tent from his dad. Jimmy Jr had plied his trade on the football field, playing for the Western Suburbs Magpies between 1934 and 1939 (59 games for a total of 50 points – four tries and 19 goals). After that he worked full-time as a journalist before stepping into his dad's shoes in 1955.

Sharman Jr would insist that his fighters' contracts forbade them using "intoxicating liquors and injurious drugs" and drunken challengers were not allowed in the ring. In terms of payment, he said he kept all their winnings until the end of the tour so they would leave with cash in their pockets. But Corris claims the Sharmans' contracts were seriously balanced in father and son's favour.

"... the hours of work exacted were long, conditions rough and the boxers had no union protection or right of appeal from the management's decisions," Corris wrote. "It is hard to imagine such a contract being legally enforceable today. It makes no mention of Sharman's responsibilities in medical matters, accommodation or manner of payment and was designed to extract the maximum effort from the fighter while giving the management the maximum protection."

Still, the Sharman tent, and others, were appealing to Aboriginal fighters. With rampant discrimination in Australia for the entire time of Sharman's operation, the tents were a way for them to earn a quid. On top of that, it was a chance to be seen as equals (of a sort) with the white men who entered their ring. And the tents also gave them the chance to take their grievances out on a white man.

Fighters like Lionel Rose and Tony Mundine came up through the boxing tent circuit. Mundine told SBS he found Sharman's tent had a professional focus. "There were nine or 10 guys on the tent, walking around, and they would match you up to make sure you'd be able to play someone similar to your height and weight," Mundine said. "And they'd always make sure you got your dollar – they'd pay you well for fighting." But Sharman Jr didn't have the most enlightened of attitudes about his Aboriginal charges, telling the *Sydney Morning Herald* in 2003 that "it's in their blood to fight". Charming.

In 1971, Sharman Jr closed up shop, the family tent killed off largely by a more enlightened approach to boxers' safety. The NSW government brought in laws that restricted boxers to one fight a week and those who were knocked out were banned from fighting for a month. Also, vehicular mobility meant families were less likely to hang around a showground all day looking for amusement. "Years ago families would go early to the show and stop there all day," Sharman Jr said. "Now they've all got motor cars. They come in at one and are gone by 4.30."

The closure of the family business wasn't a problem for Jimmy Sharman Jr's son, Jim. With an interest in theatre, Jim Sharman went to NIDA and ended up directing the stage hit *Rocky Horror Show*, and directed and co-wrote *The Rocky Horror Picture Show*.

When it comes to the recording of *Jimmy Sharman's Boxers*, this is one of a couple of "toilet tracks" on *Red Sails in the Sunset*. That is, songs where at least one of the instruments were recorded in the loo, in search of superior acoustics. In an online Q&A Gifford was asked for a *"Spinal Tap"* moment from the Tokyo sessions.

"One time Rob was experimenting with drum sounds for *Jimmy Sharman's Boxers* and he ended up in the toilets with a monitoring station and a long cable connected back to the control room," Gifford said.

"The manager Mr Hashiguchi happened to come by our studio and asked 'we have beautiful studio, why you record in toilet?'."

When *Red Sails* came out, I was no fan of this song; I especially didn't like that fact that it took up more than seven minutes of precious vinyl space. But it's a sign of good art that it changes and shows new sides of itself to you as you get older. It's like the song grows up as you do. And so, there I was, doing a bit of "homework" for the Midnight Oil reunion gig in my home town. That meant playing a few Oils CDs to reacquaint myself with the band (it had been years since I listened to any of their albums in its entirety). The *Red Sails* disc got to track five and the hairs on my arms suddenly stood and tears started welling my eyes.

In the interests of full disclosure, I'd had a few beers and may have been a bit more "emotionally susceptible".

But still, a song that was one I used to hate is now one of my favourites. Even when I listen to it sober. It's a rollercoaster ride of emotion that's more than seven minutes long and there's not a wasted second there. It kicks off that with a replication of the Sharman's beating bass drum and the traditional call to brawl of "a round or two for a pound or two".

I assume that's one of the band members impersonating Sharman (there's no credit on the album sleeve saying they sourced an original recording) but I'm not sure which one it is. If I had to guess, I'd go for Peter Garrett. From there a slow drum beat kicks in, with a sad, sparse guitar line with more space than sound. Garrett's vocals start with a shaky, almost spoken-word feel that contributes to create a feeling of tension. That tension goes up a level in the second verse; while the music stays the same Garrett lifts his vocal performance.

Two minutes in and the drumbeats get more urgent, backing great lyrics about eyes blacker than their skin and how winning doesn't make a difference to them (though evidence from some of the boxers themselves has suggested otherwise). Then comes the plea from the boxers to the crowd, asking them why they are willing to pay for the chance of seeing a black man hitting the canvas.

They wonder if there's a reason the crowds keep coming back but, they must surely know the answer has something to do with the feeling of superiority those outside the ring believe they hold over those dark-skinned men fighting inside. The chance to watch someone lay a few punches on a dark-skinned man, or maybe do some of the punching themselves, was just too good to resist. It's a point Hirst punctuates with some insistent punch-like electronic tom toms.

Garrett then tells us our protagonist is wilting, close to collapsing on the canvas, with the crowd calling on the opponent to finish the job. And we're barely halfway through the song. Fortunately, there's a short break to catch our breath and to hold the dramatic tension – which is helped by the faint cries of the crowd in the background.

But it doesn't last long. Soon the song begins to build to a climax with drumming that seems louder than before, and two guitars playing that sparse riff where there previously only seemed to be one. Soon, the question of why the locals keep coming to watch is asked, but this time in a more desperate, accusing tone. Some wailing trombone comes in, and those questions return but with a forlorn feeling behind them, as though it's pointless to ask because they will never get an answer. The song then moves to the final notes, leaving the listener wringing wet from the tension and the fate of our protagonist left on his knees remaining unstated.

Phew.

Bakerman
(Hirst)
0.51

This is a song that is the answer to a few trivia questions:

What is the shortest song recorded by Midnight Oil?

Yep, it's *Bakerman*, clocking in at just 51 seconds. To the best of my knowledge every other song Midnight Oil recorded went for at least a minute. And they put a bit of effort into it, dragging in a brass section to play for 50-something seconds. Or maybe they had the brass guys in to record something else and thought, "hey, we're paying you by the hour and we've got 51 seconds left, give this song a crack".

Which recorded Midnight Oil song actually features no members of Midnight Oil?

It's *Bakerman*, at least I think it is. There's no one credited as playing any brass on the liner notes and I'm pretty sure none of the five members are very proficient in the brassy instruments. Also, I can't hear any guitars, drums, bass, keyboards or whatever instruments the band members CAN play on that track.

What song do fans most often offer up as the worst Midnight Oil song?

Yeah, I reckon it's *Bakerman* again. I don't have any solid evidence to back this up but you just know a weird, brass-heavy instrumental that's less than a minute long isn't going to float too many people's boats. Which would mean the least favourite Oils song is on what many nominate as their least favourite Oils album. There's an odd kind of symmetry there.

There's no question *Bakerman* is an odd little beast. It's likely the most un-Midnight Oil song Midnight Oil recorded (at least until someone uncovers a long-lost Oils take on the early '80s New Romantic era). Coming across a little like theme song looking for a cartoon TV show to pair up with, it does stand out alongside some of the more serious topics. Look up anomaly in the dictionary and it'll say "see *Bakerman*".

I don't mind the song. I see it as a circuit breaker for the previous trio of songs which are about

Aboriginal people in custody (*Sleep*), nuclear annihilation (*Minutes to Midnight*), and a harrowing epic about whitey looking to pummel Aboriginal men in a boxing ring (*Jimmy Sharman's Boxers*). These days albums often tend to be a series of separate songs but back in ye olden days, there was some thought given to the track sequencing. This light ditty works well at the back end of side one, giving the listener a bit of breathing space before flipping the vinyl to side two.

Of all the songs on *Red Sails in the Sunset*, this is the one I found the least information on. And by least, I mean "next to nothing". As far as I can tell, the band remained tight-lipped as to what was going on in the studio when they recorded this. I couldn't find a single instance of any member talking about *Bakerman* – not even the songwriter Rob Hirst, who always seems more than happy to talk about anything Oils-related.

There is a demo of the song floating around on YouTube, which only serves to deepen the mystery because it is some distance from the finished product. While you can hear the melody of the demo in the closing track of side one of *Red Sails*, the demo is three times as long, contains no brass at all and it even has lyrics. Now, not only do we not know why they recorded a sub-minute brass instrumental, we also don't know how they started with a three-minute song played by the full band and ended up with a much shorter piece in which none of them appear.

That early version of *Bakerman* is one of seven demo recordings of songs that ended up making it to *Red Sails in the Sunset* – all of which are available via YouTube. The others are *Who Can Stand in the Way*, *Sleep*, *Shipyards of New Zealand*, *Minutes to Midnight*, *Kosciusko* and *Best of Both Worlds*.

Moginie has said part of his issue with *Red Sails in the Sunset* was that they went in without enough songs and had to work up a number in the studio (which he implies was not the best way to get choice tunes). These demo tapes might offer a clue as to which songs were created at the last minute – which would basically be any album track other than those seven.

So that would leave *When the Generals Talk*, *Jimmy Sharman's Boxers*, *Helps Me Helps You*, *Harrisburg* and *Bells and Horns in the Back of Beyond* as those the band bashed together in the studio.

Which is a bit confusing to be frank. Now while I freely admit a bias towards ALL the songs on *Red Sails*, I do have an opinion on which songs seemed to be late creations. *Boxers* doesn't sound like it was nailed together in the studio; for such a long song to be so well-crafted it had to be put together much earlier.

But *Generals*, that totally does. It's a fine song – but I can't help but wonder whether a song that *already* sounds like it's been disco remixed would sneak through to vinyl at any other stage in the band's career.

Bells and Horns? Yeah, I can totally see that being a studio creation. It sounds like they cobbled together bits and pieces from a few other songs to get that one. Which doesn't mean it's a bad song – especially not the "surf-western movie soundtrack" sounds in the second half.

And with all its studio effects and the Darth Vader breath as percussion (which I love by the way) *Harrisburg* surely has to be something they didn't have before they got to Tokyo. The same goes for *Helps Me Helps You*, which would be my least favourite track on the album.

As for those seven songs that were demoed, none of them are as different from their finished version as *Bakerman*. *Best of Both Worlds* has hardly changed from demo days to the finished products, even some of the Rotsey guitar wails that I'd expected he pulled out of his hat during the recording session for the album are there on the demo.

The start of the *Kosciusko* demo features the bit that ended up in the middle of the finished product – just after Garrett's "ultimatum". The jarring difference is the lack of the Rob Hirst drum-athon on the demo, which for me, is the defining characteristic of the album track.

Who Can Stand in the Way still comes with that funky bassline and the lyrics are largely the same. Even Garrett's vocal outro about emus at Pyrmont – which doesn't appear on the album's lyric sheet – is there, albeit with a far more rushed delivery. The big difference is the Hawaiian/country style twang of the guitar and what I'd bet is the sound of an odd little instrument known as a thumb piano.

Thank God the band jettisoned the cheesy "da-da-da' backing vocals that appear in the *Shipyards of New Zealand* demo. It seriously sounds like it's a Broadway show-tunes pisstake - and it's behind each of the verses. Sure, they replaced them with those breathy "ah-uhs" but, trust me, it's an improvement. Broadly speaking though, the bulk of the finished song is there in the demo version.

Sleep is a song that has undergone one of the biggest transformations. It's not a *Bakerman*-style overhaul, but it's a big step from the demo to the finished product. Gifford's slinky basswork is still there, so the underlying rhythm is the same, and the clarinet makes an appearance, but just about everything else is different. The finished intro is more jaunty, the basswork gets to stand alone rather than being wound together with an accompanying guitar, the lyrics are more fully-formed in the album version and the band has worked out an ending for the song rather than just letting the clarinet wail away over a repeating guitar riff.

Unlike *Bakerman*, you can hear how they got from the demo to the finished version. But sadly we end this chapter none the wiser about what the band was doing when they added a 51-second instrumental to *Red Sails in the Sunset*.

Side Two

Who Can Stand in the Way
(Moginie/Garrett)
4.33

The cover of *Red Sails in the Sunset* is without a doubt the most striking of all the releases in the band's catalogue. I'd go further and make the claim that it's the best album cover from an Australian artist. You see that cover and you don't forget it. People who had never heard of Midnight Oil picked up a copy of the album on the strength of that cover alone.

It's testament to the power of the image that the neither the band name or album title appears on the cover. For the most part, at least. Some later versions put the band and title at the top of the image, which to me feels like defacing a work of art. Artist and album title branding wasn't needed; you saw that cover and you simply *had* to pick it up out of the racks at the record store (yes, I'm talking about a vinyl cover. The image does lose some power shrunken down for a CD – though the colour resolution on some vinyl reissues does that image no favours).

Like all good art, the cover allows people to add their own meaning to it, to interpret it based on their own experiences. Given that the album came out in Orwell's year of 1984, where the Cold War between the USA and the USSR seemed like it could become hot at any moment, many people saw it as carrying an apocalyptic portent. With the nuclear bomb craters in the Sydney CBD, the northern approach of harbour bridge destroyed (but with the bridge and the iconic Sydney Opera House still standing so it's clear we're looking at Sydney) the message was read as "this is what could be waiting for you just around the corner.

The only problem is, that's *not* what is happening in the image at all. It's a routinely repeated myth that the *Red Sails* cover shows an image of a post-nuclear Sydney. It even appears in the liner notes that accompany the band's *Full Tank* collection; those notes claim it's a photo montage "of a future Sydney, and harbour, devastated and reduced to a giant crater by an imagined nuclear strike".

Look, there are two huge craters on either side of the harbour bridge – the opera house also sits on the rim of one of them. Ask yourself this, if a nuclear bomb exploded just a few metres from those iconic structures, how can they still be standing? And how can almost the entire cityscape in the background be untouched? The air blast from detonation should have blown them over. And what about all the water in the harbour - did the bomb obliterate it all?

Here's something else to consider: in a war nuclear bombs don't leave craters because they explode in the air, not the ground. An air burst spreads the explosive force over a wide area. Detonating it in the ground sends most of that force through the earth. The bombs at Nagasaki and Hiroshima were detonated in the air, that's why there are no bomb craters in either city. Really, the only time we saw craters from atomic bomb was during the testing when the bombs were mounted on scaffolds just metres from the ground. In those instances, the aim was to see if the bomb would explode, not to cause the maximum amount of devastation.

If it's not a shot of Sydney post-apocalypse, then what's going on? During an interview with a US TV show host who was prone to talking over his guests, Garrett managed to get out an explanation. The talky host says it depicts Sydney after the "holocaust"

"It's not after the holocaust actually," Garrett says. "The buildings are still there."

Then the host starts rambling on about how "they say everything in the centre of an explosion survives", before telling a story about guys bundling themselves up in a boxful of dynamite and then exploding it. Garrett, who looks like he's wishing the guy would shut up, finally gets to clear things up.

"The idea here is that it's the desert taking over the city as much as anything else," he says.

The cover was created by Japanese artist Tsunehisa Kimura, and one of the themes of much of his work was juxtaposing the urban and natural worlds. Another work is a photomontage of a waterfall flowing across the top of a cityscape and down the side of a skyscraper (which also appeared on album covers by the Climax Blues Band and Australian band Cut Copy). There are also images of battleships sailing in fields and rollercoasters set up on the edge of a waterfall.

It's also a theme reflected in the closing lyrics of the song *Who Can Stand in the Way* (the ones that don't appear in the lyric sheet). They talk of the bush grass known as spinifex rolling into Sydney, the desert intruding on the northern suburb of Gladesville and emus popping up at Pyrmont not far from the Sydney Harbour Bridge. It's the bush overtaking the city.

You ask me, that's a far more pleasant theme than Sydney being attacked by a giant testicle. According to Hirst – and he claims to have the artwork at home to prove it – that was the part of Kimura's original vision. He told the story in a speech for the opening of a 2013 exhibition of imaginary album covers.

"For our 1984 album *Red Sails in the Sunset*, for example," Hirst said, "some of the band members loved one of the first cover art suggestions; a depiction of Sydney Harbour emptied out by an enormous, fiery testicle, which had apparently plummeted from the sky like a meteorite and left a barren wasteland of red dirt and craters. Other band members however, rejected this first draft of the cover art. They suspected that the Kimura-san, the famous Japanese photomontage artist commissioned for the job, had been a little too generous in his regular self-applications of sake."

Looking at the finished cover, you have to wonder if Kimura-san didn't just tinker with that testicle a little to make it look more fiery and less anatomical. For there is a big ball on the cover, right near the harbour bridge.

The subject matter of the song *Who Can Stand in the Way* is effectively the opposite message of the album cover. Rather than the wilderness taking over the city, the song laments suburbia's steady encroachment into the natural environment.

That's a process that started in January 1788 according to the second verse, where Garrett takes the perspective of an Aboriginal person standing on Dobroyd Point watching the white sails of the First Fleet enter the harbour. And from there, as the lyrics say, we just carried on raping and gouging through to the present day.

The title of the song suggests a question, though the absence of a question mark at the end is telling. It suggests it's really more of a statement than anything else, and that the band likely already know the answer. As more than 200 years of European settlement, it seems that pretty much no one wants to stand in the way if there's some bucks to be had.

Kosciusko
(Hirst/Moginie)
4.40

Just so you know, Mt Kosciuszko isn't actually named for the person who discovered it (yes, when I say "discovered" I mean a white man – surely the native population knew the highest mountain in the country was there long before we did). Not that it would have made the mountain's name any easier to spell – the guy who discovered it had the surname of Strzelecki.

He chose to name the mountain after a man who would never see the mountain, a man who would never even set foot in Australia.

Because that's just the person to name a country's biggest mountain after, isn't it? Incidentally, Strzelecki would later get his own mountain – in the Northern

Territory. A part of Australia he, rather appropriately, it would seem, appears never to have visited himself

The Kosciuszko in question was Tadeusz Kosciuszko, a hero in Poland (where Strzelecki was from) and in the United States too. He studied at the Warsaw military academy but, when he fell in love with his boss' daughter and tried to elope, dad had him beaten up.

That prompted Tad's flight to France, and ultimately the United States where he got tied up in the American War of Independence. He soon was made a colonel, the US leaders keen to use his knowledge of engineering. To that end, they got him to devise the fortifications at a range of places, including West Point.

He saw no action until the final year of the war, where he became involved in some small skirmishes. After the war, he returned to Poland – just in time to catch the Russian invasion of his country. He went into the field to defend his country and won every battle he fought in until the king surprisingly gave in to the Russians.

That sat poorly with Kosciuszko who became part of a group hell-bent on ending Russian rule in Poland. The uprising that bears his name was an undeniable failure, both for the Polish people – the Russians massacred thousands of them – and for Kosciuszko himself who was wounded and captured.

He languished in jail until the death of Catherine the Great saw a change in relations with Poland. The new Tzar Paul I pardoned Kosciuszko, who headed to the United States for a number of years before returning to Europe again and getting into a few arguments with Napoleon.

Aged 71 he fell off his horse and died; more than 20 years later a Pole named Strzelecki would climb the highest mountain in a country the war hero had never visited and name it after him.

The eagle-eyed reader may notice that the spelling of the man's surname and the Midnight Oil song aren't the same. The spelling used to be the anglicised Koscuisko until the NSW Geographical Names Board in 1997 officially adopted the proper spelling of the man's name. The version of *Red Sails in the Sunset* that comes in the Full Tank collection contains an explanation of this decision, to allay listener's confusions lest they think the band can't spell properly.

Now, all of the above may seem irrelevant, given the song *Koscuisko* isn't about the mountain at all. Which is something I only discovered while researching this book. Before then, I just assumed it was about the mountain. The song was named after it, how could it *not* be about the mountain.

It wasn't until I checked the names of the towns mentioned in the song and went, "hang on, these places are miles away from Kosciuszko – they're not even in the same state". So it turns out the mountain is name-checked as a reference to how long the Aboriginal population has been here – at least that's the way I interpret it. In a piece for *Spin* magazine in August 1985 journalist Bill Wolfe suggested the song was one of several (*Sleep* is another) that was inspired by a visit in 1984 to play a concert at an Aboriginal settlement in northwest Queensland.

Songwriter Hirst has said the song is about the conflict between black and white. "For me it was the first writing I'd done about the interaction between Australia's indigenous people and European Australians," he said. "*Kosciusko* was the first time I got onto an album this idea that somewhere down the track there would have to be some kind of a confrontation if not understanding between Australia's First Nation people and European Australians."

This is the second of two songs on *Red Sails* where Hirst sings lead. While *Generals* comes first in terms of the track order, it was *Kosciusko* that the band recorded first. In the band bio *Beds are Burning*, producer Nick Launay said *Kosciusko* was the first time he'd heard Hirst sing lead. With Garrett disappearing to do his political thing, the band needed a vocal track so they could work on the song – so Hirst sang what was apparently meant to be a guide vocal. Garrett was supposed to turn up at some stage and, when he did, he'd hear that lyric and be able to fit into the space the instruments had left for him.

Well, Garrett did turn up but, according to Launay, didn't see the need to record over the top of Hirst's effort (though he is there in the backing vocals). He wouldn't have been unfamiliar with the tune – he sang the lead on the demo version where it started life as a country tune. The song would never have been a live favourite had it not undergone a few changes. And one change in particular – turning the thing into a four-minute drum solo.

"In retrospect," he said in Kruger's *Songwriters Speak*, "the obvious thing was it was like a fucking drum solo with vocals over the top and studded with a nice acoustic thing and everything else was blown out of the water."

Combined with the duty of singing lead, playing this is definitely a job for an energetic young drummer (has any other drummer had biceps like Hirst? No wonder he loved wearing sleeveless shirts), which is why on the *Great Circle* reunion tour, the tune was stripped back with Hirst playing on a cocktail kit because he could play the full kit or sing but not both.

Which is both understandable and a bit of a shame. Because *Kosciusko* just doesn't feel the same without that thundering, rolling peal of drums. At times it sounds like Hirst has brought every drum he'd ever owned into the studio and is endeavouring to hit each of them at least once before the song finishes. That's the reason this song has been so popular with fans for so long. Everyone loves a song where the drummer thrashes it out.

Aside from the drums, drums and more drums, the other thing that stands out are the drunken musicians at the end. The story goes that the band got a very, very professional string quartet in to play that outro. Because they were very, very professional, they laid down a note-perfect, flawless piece. Which really didn't work because it made the band look bad. "We got Japanese string players in and they played it perfectly," Hirst said on Music Max's *The Artist's Story*.

"We thought 'it's good and it's perfect but it's making us sound really sloppy. "So we asked the studio manager to administer his finest sake, which was handed around the string players. And then handed around again."

After about 10 minutes of boozing (or whatever it is you do when getting drunk on sake), Midnight Oil had brought the quartet down to their level. And they got the "sloppy" take they needed.

Helps Me Helps You
(Hirst/Moginie)
3.23

It was soon after the release of *Red Sails in the Sunset* that Garrett announced his now-legendary tilt at the federal Senate. So, with that in mind, it would seem that *Helps Me Helps You* takes on a greater significance. It's obviously about the dark art of politics, with Garrett himself singing from the point of view of a self-interested politician happy to do whatever works for him. Though you could mount a case that "self-interested politician" is a bit of a tautology.

Here's a guy who is about to become a politician singing about all the problems that are so often part and parcel of politics. Garrett didn't write the song, that was Hirst and Moginie's work. Were they having a sly dig at their bandmate over his new potential vocation? It would be kind of funny if they were, but

I tend to doubt it. The subject matter of the song is largely in line with the sort of issues the band was tackling as their political focus increased.

Besides, it's unclear exactly when the band actually knew he was running. While there is some suggestion they figured something was up while recording *Red Sails* in Tokyo from June to August, nothing really seems to have happened until that gap between when the band returned to Australia and the release of the album.

Journalist and band confidant Andrew McMillan wrote a piece for *RAM* in early November 1984 that suggests the newly formed Nuclear Disarmament Party approach didn't occur until September, after the band's return. That was when Garrett called for a band meeting.

"It was a classic Oils meeting that seemed to last for hours," Hirst told McMillan. "But after all, this is something that – as a band – we've been heading towards for a long time.

"My reaction was, you know, obviously the issue and the election couldn't wait and that he should go full steam into it …"

In the 1986 book *Pay to Play* Garrett confirms that the approach came after the band touched down in Sydney. The decision to accept the offer really sees the band at a crossroads. For years they'd been struggling to get to the peak of the rock mountain and they'd finally made it (though hindsight shows the next album took them to even higher altitudes). Just when things are looking good, the band's irreplaceable lead singer (and he is – how do you replace a gangly balding giant behind the mic stand? Garrett is the key visual of the band) decides to head off and do something else. Despite the fact that his departure "sounds like an ending" (see what I did there?) for the band, they let him go do his thing.

Sure, if they'd said no, and made Garrett stay his itchy feet would likely soon have been a huge pain in the butt to deal with. Still, it's quite a selfless gesture for the four guys in the band who *aren't* interested running for the Senate to let the one guy who is give it a crack, even if it could mean the end of the band.

And that was a very real possibility. As the recent *Midnight Oil: 1984* documentary showed, Garrett was burning the candle at both ends during the election campaign. He'd head off early to do some campaigning, then turn up to whichever venue the band was playing that night, flog himself senseless and collapse on the floor backstage. Then he'd get up and do it all again the next day. There is no way that sort of lifestyle was sustainable in the long term. Besides, the electorate is a funny thing, they'd want him to give all his efforts to the job and not bugger off to play gigs here, there and everywhere or even head off for months to record an album in Tokyo.

On that band-ending score, the band themselves never seem 100 per cent sure it would all be sweet after Garrett left. Hirst in particular has chopped and changed over the years. When McMillan asked him whether a Garrett win would "dissipate the energy of the band", he responded with "no, quite the contrary actually. In fact this will be, to most Oil people who know our history, the final consolidation of where we stand on the issue". In the Music Max doco *The Artist's Story* he said, "There was never any suggestion that the band was going to end", a claim he reiterated in the *Midnight Oil: 1984* doco.

But in the book *Beds are Burning*, he sings a different tune: "I was concerned about the future of the band because I felt a band that had to rehearse between Senate sittings might be a band that quickly folded in frustration."

Pete Gifford thought it could really happen. "We supported him," he said in *Beds are Burning*, "but we'd made plans if he won his seat to the point where we were quite prepared to lose the band. We knew if Pete got his seat then "Goodbye Midnight Oil' as we know it."

The Nuclear Disarmament Party had only started in June 1984, a few months before the band returned home. The founder was a Canberra doctor by the name of Michael Denborough and the initial policies were to close all foreign military bases in Australia, refuse to allow nuclear weapons to be placed on Australian soil or travel through Australian waters and put an end to uranium mining.

Garrett's arrival caused anger in some segments of the party. He was approached by the NSW committee, who figured a glamour candidate was needed. Denborough was considerably pissed off about this for he viewed the No1 spot on NSW Senate ticket as his right as founder of the party. After a close vote Denborough was forced to vacate the No1 spot so Garrett could contest the position. At a heated general meeting on October 7 – which was plugged on Triple J to try and get as many Garrett supporters in the door – Denborough arrived with his own contingent. According to *Half-Life*, a book on the party by Gillian Fisher (who ended up No2 on the ticket) Garrett came first "by a hefty margin". "The Denborough contingent simply got up and left," Fisher wrote.

Garrett's win on the ballot paper made the newspapers the next day. *The Sydney Morning Herald* reported "he would temporarily leave his group if elected". "I'm willing to put my music on ice for a while," he said in a brief story.

A day later, Prime Minister Bob Hawke called an election for December 1, so Garrett and his team got moving. That he and other newcomers with experience handling the media took control did get a few noses out of joint, Fisher wrote, until they realised the party was "dead lucky" to have them on board. Garrett sensed the tension, he told Fisher; "I was aware of some disquiet and perhaps some resentment about the fact that we had already taken over the organisation and the running of the campaign and the political and media focus to some extent." But he said it didn't bother him; the importance of the nuclear issue held sway over "any inevitable jostlings of people".

In the early days of the campaign Garrett had to face that question of what happens to the band. "Midnight Oil will go on playing and I may have some part to play in that, but I want to be considered a serious and legitimate candidate," he told the *Herald*'s Richard Glover. "I want people to understand the issues and then to believe that by getting involved they can do something about it."

But that didn't mean he would quit the band before the election. The NDP launched the campaign at Mrs Macquarie's Chair in mid-November at the ungodly hour of 6am, with a collection of journalists raising their microphones over their head to reach the mouth of a standing Garrett. From there, he had to play a series of dates for the *Red Sails* tour at night and stalk the campaign trail during the day. In *Half-Life* Garrett told Fisher the key concern was "Can I keep going without falling over altogether?" "I was using the Midnight Oil tour – they were paying for the airfares – to do the other work when I wasn't on stage or sound-[checking] or whatever," he said.

Initially, the upstart party led by a bald rock singer wasn't given much chance. As the December 1 election drew nearer, the incumbent Labor party started treating the NDP as a threat, largely because the newcomers had been drawing away the major party's left-wing voters. Hawke began attacking the party for an inability to express any policy aside from the anti-nuclear stance. Garrett's response was, well, less than inspiring – "It is unfair to expect a party that has basically only been going for six weeks to answer all those questions before the election because it is not going to be able to do that," he told the media before promising more detail at some stage the following week.

Ahead of the election, the Labor and Liberal parties agreed to swap preferences. The vagaries of the Australian electoral system are too difficult to explain here, but a preference deal (preferences are effectively a second choice if the voter's first choice doesn't win) is a way of shutting out a third party. And that's what happened - while Garrett polled a high primary vote of 9.7 per cent; other parties sent their second choice votes away from the singer.

Still, it went down to the wire for the seventh and final NSW Senate seat. It wasn't until January 8, five weeks after the election, that Democrat Colin Mason was announced as the winner; at that point Garrett was the only other candidate still in the race. Mason had pulled in more than 460,000 preference votes, substantially more than the 311,000-plus votes that went to Garrett.

The singer chose to look on the bright side. "I think we have had a great victory. We took disarmament and made it a major election issue. I am not disappointed not to become a senator in the parliament and I am thrilled that so many people have voted for me."

He would only be a part of the Nuclear Disarmament Party for a few more months. In late April he, Jo Valentine (the only NDP candidate to win at the 1984 election) and others walked out of the national conference alleging it had been taken over by the Socialist Workers Party (SWP). I am not opposed to socialism as a whole," he told the *Sydney Morning Herald*. "What I am opposed to is the ideology and tactics used by the SWP. They are experienced, they have a long history of entering other groups to build up their own numbers, and they're good at it."

A month after the walkout they would form another party – Peace and Nuclear Disarmament Action – which went under the oh-so-cute acronym PANDA. Over time, Garrett would put forward the view that he was pleased not to have won that 1984 Senate seat. "I was elated to lose," he told US *People* magazine in 1990. "Otherwise it would have been hard for us to keep playing." A comment that very much sounds like the election win would have killed off the band.

Of course, years later Garrett's political ambitions would see the end of the band in 2002. "The last 25 years have been extremely fulfilling for me, and I leave with the greatest respect for the whole of Midnight Oil," he said in a statement on the band's website. "But it is time for me to move on and immerse myself in those things which are of deep concern to me and which I have been unable to fully apply myself to up to now."

He won the seat of Kingsford Smith for the Labor Party in 2004 and became a minister after the party's election victory in 2007. He would be the subject of a lot of criticism for selling out and never really seemed able to put forward a decent explanation for his nine years as a Labor politician.

Four years after leaving government – 15 years after the band officially ended – the band reformed for the *Great Circle* tour. So maybe a 1984 election *wouldn't* have ended the band, we just would have had to wait more than a decade for the next tour. Which is the next worst thing if you're a fan.

As an aside, speaking of reformations in later years, the younger Peter Garrett was deadset against them. In 1986 he told Helen Thomas in *Pay to Play* he had no desire to be onstage in his 40s. "When I look at people like David Bowie and Mick Jagger, Pete Townshend, Bob Dylan and all those characters," he said, "I think those who have tried to continue living on the myth of their youthful performances and creativity have become more than caricatures – they've become semi-tragic figures."

Wonder how that younger Garrett would feel now.

Harrisburg
(Moginie/Kevans)
3.48

Three Mile Island isn't actually three miles long. At best it's a little over two miles in length. Its name derives from the distance to another point – some sources say the island is three miles downriver from the town of Middleton, another claims that's the distance you'd have to travel if you were leaving the island and heading for Harrisburg International Airport. That second explanation seems a bit odd to me. The island was there long before the airport – why name it after the distance to a landmark that hadn't been built?

At least Three Mile Island is *actually* an island. It sits in the Susquehanna River, with towns a few hundred metres away on both of the riverbanks. Neither of those are called Harrisburg – that city is 22 kilometres upriver from the island. These days the term Three Mile Island is shorthand for an event on March 28, 1979, rather than the place itself. That event would be an accident that effectively killed the nuclear power industry. In the wake of the incident, planned nuclear power plants around the world were cancelled and another plant wouldn't be constructed until 2012. Meanwhile, the second nuclear plant on Three Mile Island (yes, there were two of them – the plant takes up most of the space on the island) resumed operations in 1985, creating electricity for towns in Pennsylvania. Exelon, the company that owns the plant, announced it would close down in 2019.

The accident in 1979 was basically an overheating of the nuclear fuel inside the reactor. That was caused by a relief valve that opened to relieve pressure in the reactor becoming stuck and staying open when pressure returned to normal. However the instrument panel told the operators it *was* closed – that was a problem because the coolant that sat around the nuclear fuel and regulated its temperature was flowing out of that valve.

"There was no instrumentation that showed how much water covered the core," according to the United States Nuclear Regulatory Commission. "As a result plant staff assumed that as long as the pressurizer water level was high, the core was properly covered with water. As alarms rang and warning lights flashed, the operators did not realise that the plant was experiencing a loss of coolant accident."

A lack of coolant meant the fuel pellets began to melt, though the exterior of the plant stayed intact as did the fuel containment unit. This is why, technically, what happened at Three Mile Island wasn't a full meltdown – in that situation, the fuel eats through the protective shields and gets outside the plant.

Of concern at Three Mile Island was several small releases of radioactive gas that were detected offsite and the corresponding risk to the community. While the fuel itself was stabilised later on the day of the accident, the next day there was a significant release of radiation. Pennsylvania governor Richard Thornburgh spoke with Nuclear Regulatory Commission (NRC) chair Joseph Hendrie about evacuation plans. They agreed those "most vulnerable to radiation" – in the words of the NRC – would need to leave.

"Thornburgh announced that he was advising pregnant women and pre-school age children within a five-mile radius of the plant to leave the area," the NRC said. A day later the radius was extended to 20 miles and around 140,000 residents left the area, which was less than a third of the population in the evacuation zone. On Sunday, April 1, some Catholic priests granted general absolution during mass. A few days later the Federal Reserve sent extra cash supplies to banks in the area, as people had withdrawn large sums in preparation for leaving.

Most of the evacuees returned to their homes within a few weeks and testing by a number of different groups found the gas release was unlikely to have had much of an effect on people's health.

It had a huge effect on the health of the nuclear power industry. Though the reactor itself was cleaned and closed down, the fear it generated caused widespread community concern about the safety of nuclear reactors. Anti-nuclear protests were mounted and orders for new plants were cancelled.

What may have also fueled the swing against nuclear power was the release – just 12 days before the accident – of the movie *The China Syndrome*. In the movie journalists film a major accident at a power plant and discover a safety cover-up. In an echo of Three Mile Island, faulty equipment leads to the coolant in the reactor reaching dangerously low levels.

The title of the film itself is a reference to a nuclear meltdown, where the fuel rods burn a hole through the Earth all the way to China (something that couldn't actually happen).

In terms of Midnight Oil trivia, *Harrisburg* is one answer to the question, "name a song where a songwriting credit is given to someone who is not a member of the band?". There is just one other correct answer – *Sins of Omission* off the *Breathe* album where producer Malcolm Burn gets a songwriting credit (the occasional credit to someone with the surname of "Stevens" may initially throw you, until you remember bassist Bones Hillman's real name is Wayne Stevens).

By my count the band recorded 127 songs over 13 albums and EPs. So to have just two of those songs where some outside assistance was given is pretty impressive. It really speaks to the songwriting strength that is within the band.

When it comes to *Harrisburg* that outside influence is Australian poet Denis Kevans. His poem of the same name appeared in a self-published collection called *The Great Prawn War*. Because it was self-published, it's a hard book to find so many Midnight Oil fans aren't sure just how much of the song was taken from the poem. If they have to hazard a guess, they suggest it must only be a line or two, because why would a band so stacked with songwriters need to take any more than that from someone else?

It's an understandable assumption, but also a false one. Of the 127 words that make up the song, 84 of them come from Kevans' poem. That includes all the most powerful lines; the chorus about the plant melting down, the stuff getting into your body and how you cannot get it out. The only non-Kevans lines are the first four and the one at the end about the drawn curtains.

That the song features mostly Kevans' words led to a rumour the band had to be threatened with legal action before giving him credit and, therefore, royalties. I could find no direct mention of such a lawsuit – and you'd think an instance of Midnight Oil being sued for stealing someone else's work would definitely get coverage. Also, the early pressings of *Red Sails in the Sunset* all carry the Moginie/Kevans credit for *Harrisburg* on the label. It's hard to imagine an intensely left-wing, right-on, supporting-all-the-worthy causes band like Midnight Oil would think "hey, let's rip off this guy's poem. It's not as if anyone will notice". All of which leads me to conclude the lawsuit is simply a myth.

Harrisburg is one of the more unusual songs on an unusual album. It may even take the title of the most unusual from *Bakerman*, purely because of length. *Bakerman* is only 51 seconds long. *Harrisburg*, at 3.58 is four times as long and that means it's stranger for longer. I should make it clear that I don't see strangeness equating to badness. Yes, *Harrisburg* is strange, but I still like it.

I like that odd Darth Vader breath used as percussion, though I wasn't able to work out whose breath it was. But I'd guarantee it's not Quiet Man Rotsey. In fact, I'm not sure he appears on this track all. I'm damned if I can hear any guitar work. But back to the breathing – I find it adds an eeriness to the track and the fact we hear it right up front really sets the mood for a song dealing with suburban exposure to radioactive materials. And then those keyboards that come in at the start, man, they're spooky. Indeed the keyboard use throughout – both electric and old-school – are quite effective at setting a slightly malevolent mood.

But those cartoon-like sound effects that come in after the first chorus, I don't about know those. They nearly mess up the song.

Bells and Horns in the Back of Beyond
(Midnight Oil)
3.14

Songwriting can really create a schism in a band with those who write the songs on one side of the chasm and those who don't on the other. You see, when a record company would pay for an album to be recorded, it's not an act of charity, it's a loan. They want that money back – and they get it by claiming the sales royalties (aka "mechanical royalties") from the album. So the band members don't see a cent of those royalties until they've paid back what they owe.

It's a very different story when it comes to those who write the songs. They also get songwriting royalties, and the record companies aren't able to get their hands on that money. So while the band as a whole isn't making any royalties, the songwriter definitely is. And if you're not the songwriter, seeing that guy getting the cash while you still have to work a part-time job to earn money can very quickly become a source of friction.

In the interests of harmony, some songwriters will share their royalties with the rest of the band, whether it be an even split or based on a percentage of total royalties. Perhaps unsurprisingly, Midnight Oil is one of those bands. When it comes to songwriting, bassplayer Peter Gifford's name doesn't crop up all that often. B*ells and Horns in the Back of Beyond* is the only *Red Sails* song he's credited with. And there was only one song on *10-1* that bore his name as well – *Somebody's Trying to Tell Me Something.* He got one credit each on the other two albums he recorded with the band, but was credited as a songwriter on all eight of the songs on the *Bird Noises* and *Species Deceases* EPs.

He had far less of a hand in the work of songwriting than Hirst and Moginie but they didn't leave him out in the cold. "I am not a songwriter and had no discernable input at concept or lyric level," Gifford said. "But we worked up a lot of material in the rehearsal room or studio so many songs were collective efforts to some degree. Thanks predominantly to the generosity of the heavy hitters

Hirst/Moginie, I receive a small percentage of songwriting royalties across all the songs on which I played."

When it came to songwriting it was those heavy hitters who did most of the work. Either they brought the starting points of songs to the band or – mainly in Moginie's case – came equipped with complete demos with everyone's parts fleshed out. "Jim has for years, right from the very beginning actually," Hirst told Kruger for *Songwriters Speak*, "delivered entire demos, some of which are remarkably unchanged after Midnight Oil has a go at them."

At this stage, Rotsey would turn on his bullshit detector and politely steer the pair away from the ideas that don't work. "There is no way of pushing something through if Martin doesn't like it," Hirst told band biographer Dodshon for *Beds are Burning*. Then Garrett would often come in with lyrical ideas, sometimes just as he was walking up to the mic to record the song. "This actually made some of the recordings incredibly stressful for the writers," Hirst told Kruger. "And so the credit there would be the lyrics that Pete added on that day."

Though being the singer singing the songs would later cause Garrett some angst when he entered politics, because he wasn't sticking true to "his" words.

Wrote journalist David Leser for the *Good Weekend* magazine "Like millions of other Australians, I'd clung to the romantic fiction of Peter Garrett remaining faithful to his songs, despite not having written most of the lyrics." That makes you cut Garrett a bit of slack when it comes to revising the lyrics of Hirst and Moginie; if you were going to have people thinking every word out of your mouth was your own and not written by someone else, you might want to try and tinker with the more contentious lines.

In the same article Labor Finance Minister Lindsay Tanner, who served with Garrett in government, pointed out it was perhaps naive to hold the tall bald guy to the words he sang back then. "It's not the 1980s anymore," Tanner said. "Whether it is Peter or not, it's absurd to take the lyrics from a song in 1984 and then compare the singer's view of the world 25 years later with those lyrics, without taking into account that we don't live in 1984 anymore."

The phrase "Bells and Horns in the Back of Beyond" comes from a *10-1* era demo written by Moginie and Garrett called *Ghost of the Roadhouse*. Moginie described it in 2014 as "a quaint little song in a way, very Australian and I think it has historical value." But he didn't think it warranted a spot on their breakthrough album – "No, it shouldn't have been released", he said.

Bells and Horns, The *Red Sails* song begat by *Ghost of the Roadhouse*, is an odd beast. It's almost like two different songs joined together right at the mid-point. It starts out as a gentle lament for Australian summers past, then it segues into what I like to think of as the theme for some surf film-cowboy western flick, complete with the return of those breathy Darth Vader noises from *Harrisburg*.

One thing that has long bugged me about this song is right there in the first two lines. For the out-of-towners, Central is the main train station in Sydney. That's where our protagonist is waiting to take the presumed object of his affections home.

The odd thing is the train they appear to be waiting for is the Southern Aurora, which was an overnighter that travelled between Sydney and Melbourne. The set-up sounds like a couple heading home after a date but waiting for that train suggests one of them lives in Melbourne. That's a long way to come for a date.

Shipyards of New Zealand
(Moginie/Garrett)
5.50

If the band had stuck more closely to the demo version of this song then we'd end up with something resembling a kitschy show tune. In the final version, there are harmonies that sound to me like sighs, run through some sort of effect that make them sound both relaxing and exhausted at the same time (well, that's how they sound to me).

On the demo version, those sighs are replaced with (presumably) Hirst and Gifford singing a jaunty "da-da-da, da-dah", accompanied by Hirst tapping on the hi-hat – which actually sounds like he's clicking his fingers along with the beat. Every time I hear this version, I can't help but picture Hirst and Gifford standing around one of those big old-fashioned microphones singing the vocals while wearing straw boaters, waistcoats and bow ties. And I am so glad they ditched them in favour of the sighs.

On the other side of the equation, I reckon they might have been better served keeping the original groove from the demo that underlies the vocals about getting lost and confused rather that the final version. The latter version is alright, with its mixture of rock and almost-orchestral moments, but the demo version, man it kills.

It starts off around the three-minute mark – where Garrett espouses his wish to fly – with Gifford locked into a great groove that drives the song along. Then those "get lost/get confused" vocals come in followed by some sparing guitar riffs that soon get bigger and build on top of that groove and vocals. It all creates a real uplift for the listener and would have seen the album finish on a high note.

The *Red Sails* demo tapes that contain this version of *Shipyards of New Zealand* also feature three songs that didn't make the grade.

One is an anti-nuclear tune called *I Want to Live Here*. It's a more straightforward number that doesn't sound like it would have fit on the *Red Sails* album, and it boasts an underwhelming, somewhat trite chorus.

Still, there are bits of the song worth saving; which is just what they did. The guitar riff that opens the song ended up on the next album as part of *Bullroarer*, while Hirst took the chorus melody and reused it in *New York, New York (Someone's Singing in the Street)*, the first single for his Ghostwriters solo project. And both those songs are better than the one that indirectly gave them birth.

Nothing is Easy is a Midnight Oil goes country sound that has some potential but the band didn't seem to agree. It seems Rotsey wasn't there for the demo recording of the last song, *Parking Station Blues* for there is no guitar on it. There is some piano, so presumably Moginie was. So it's likely this was a song in the very early stages of growth; pity it didn't go further because it's got a supremely sexy bass riff from Gifford.

When it comes to the ideas behind *Shipyards* I found this the most impenetrable song on *Red Sails in the Sunset*. I reckon I spent more time poring over the lyrics to this song than any other across these two albums, trying to prise some meaning from them. I looked up "cavalcades" on the internet, worked out what a "spreader" was, knew heading west from New Zealand had you heading to Australia, pondered whether the "factory made" line meant the narrator was a thing, rather than a person and searched through Charlton Heston's filmography for instances of stone-casting.

But none of it helped in the slightest. I went so far as to ask Google "what is *Shipyards of New Zealand* about?". For something that's supposed to be the font of all internet wisdom, Google was spectacularly unhelpful. I reckon the only two people who know what this is all about are the songwriters Moginie and Garrett – and they don't seem to be talking. I couldn't find even a single instance of them or anyone else talking about this song.

Which leads me to take drastic action and just make up something. Well, that's being a bit flippant; what I'm doing is more taking an educated guess. There's a possibility this song is at least in some way about the New Zealand declaration that nuclear-powered or nuclear-armed ships were banned from the country's ports. It happened in 1984 – the same year *Red Sails* was recorded. That year the opposition Labour Party proposed legislation that would ban such ships from entering New Zealand territorial waters, outlaw the dumping of radioactive waste in that zone and not allow New Zealanders "to manufacture, acquire, possess or have any control over any nuclear explosive device". It's likely no one had any issue with that last one. Buy many people also had no issue with the nuclear ship ban; a 1984 poll found 58 per cent were opposed to visits by US ships (who were the only nuclear warships visiting).

With a majority of only one, the ruling National Party called a snap election for July 1984 (when PM Robert Muldoon announced the early election on TV while he was visibly drunk). That sudden election ended up being a mistake; they lost 10 seats and government to the Labour Party and its leader David Lange.

He took the anti-nuclear policy with him and it became the stance of the country. Because the United States had a policy of refusing to acknowledge whether any ship was carrying nuclear weapons, it effectively meant all US ships were refused access. In response, the United States suspended its obligations to New Zealand under the ANZUS (Australia-New Zealand-United States) treaty.

The first such ban happened in February 1985, when the USS Buchanan was refused entry on the basis it was capable of launching nuclear depth charges. The United States saw the action as anti-American, stating New Zealand was a friend but not an ally. But Lange refused to back down, a stance which many New Zealanders took as a sign of their country's sovereignty and independence. It's also a policy that later New Zealand governments continued, many of which have had a designated Minister for Disarmament and Arms Control.

Now I'm well aware there is precious little in the lyrics that seem to refer to this event, unless "Charlton Heston" is taken to be a reference to the United States' response to the New Zealand decision – and even that's a stretch. Really, it's only the song title that suggests its origin is in the nuclear-free harbours, though I'm buggered if I can work out any other meaning behind it.

But the band has never made a habit of spelling everything out in their songs. And what better way to end what is an unusual, strange, odd yet thoroughly enthralling album?

Acknowledgements

When writing a book about the work of a band, it makes sense to thank them for creating it. So cheers to (in alphabetical order) Peter Garrett, Pete Gifford, Rob Hirst, Jim Moginie and Martin Rotsey. *Sounds Like an Ending* would also not have been possible without the efforts of all the writers and journalists, whose work I called on. Particular thanks goes to Mark Dodshon for his band biography *Beds Are Burning* and Debbie Kruger for her endlessly fascinating book *Songwriters Speak* (if you love music, you have to read it).

There's a very, very, *very* dedicated group of Midnight Oil fans known as the Powderworkers. I'd joined their Facebook page while researching the book and found the site – and the people – to be quite the font of information. If I wasn't sure of something, it was simply a matter of posting a question to the group and I'd have an answer – sometimes literally within minutes. Thanks guys.

For several of my books, I've asked authors far more well-known than me to supply a cover blurb where they say nice things. And no one has yet knocked me back, which shows you how wonderful writers are. This time around Jeff Apter and Stuart Coupe were gracious enough to say very nice things about *Sounds Like an Ending* and let me put those words on the cover. Jeff even supplied the foreword to the book without even being asked. Which marks them down as top blokes in my book.

Finally, a big heartfelt thanks to Kim and Josie, who put up with me spending weekends holed away in the study rather than doing fun stuff with them. I promise a whole lot of writing-free weekends from here on in.

Bibliography

BOOKS

Bongiorno, Frank, *The Eighties: The Decade That Transformed Australia*, Black Inc, 2015

Broome, Richard, 'Theatres of Power: Tent Boxing circa 1910-1970', published in *Aboriginal History Volume 20*, 1996

Collis, Ian, *The A to Z of Rugby League Players*, New Holland, 2018

Corris, Peter, *Lords of the Ring: A History of Prize-fighting in Australia*, Cassell Australia, 1980

Cross, Roger, and, Hudson, Avon, *Beyond Belief – The British Bomb Tests: Australia's Veterans Speak Out*, Wakefield Press, 2005

Dodshon, Mark, *Beds Are Burning*, Penguin, 2005

Downing, Taylor, *1983: The World at the Brink*, Little Brown, 2018

Fischer, Gillian, *Half-Life: The NDP Peace Protest and Party Politics*, State Library of NSW Press, 1995

Garrett, Peter, *Big Blue Sky*, Allen & Unwin, 2015
Garrett, Peter, *Political Blues*, Hodder and Stoughton, 1987
Gray, Mike, and, Rosen, Ira, *The Warning: Accident at Three Mile Island*, WW Norton, 2003

Hirst, Rob, *Willie's Bar and Grill*, Pan McMillan, 2012
Hoffman, David E, *The Dead Hand: The Untold Story of the Cold War Arms Race and its Dangerous Legacy*, Doubleday, 2010
Hutchinson, Tracee, *Your Name's on the Door*, ABC Books, 1992

Jones, Nate, *Able Archer 83*, The New Press, 2016

Kevans, Denis, *The Great Prawn War and Other Poems*, self-published, 1982
Kruger, Debbie, *Songwriters Speak*, Limelight Press, 2005

Lawrence, Michael, *Midnight Oil*, Melbourne Publishing, 2016
Leser, David, *The Whites of Their Eyes*, Allen & Unwin, 1999

McMillan, Andrew, *Strict Rules*, Hachette, 2017
Milson, Wendy and Thomas, Helen, *Pay to Play: Tales of the Australian Rock Industry*, Penguin, 1986

Schlosser, Eric, *Command and Control*, Penguin, 2013
Street, Andrew P, *The Long and Winding Way to the Top*, Allen & Unwin, 2017

Tynan, Elizabeth, *Atomic Thunder: The Maralinga Story*, New South 2016

Walker, Frank, *Maralinga*, Hachette, 2014
Walker, J Samuel, *Three Mile Island*, University of California Press, 2004
Warhaft, Sally (ed), *Well May We Say… The Speeches That Made Australia*, Text Publishing, 2014
Wells, HG, *The HG Wells Collection*, Arcturus Publishing, 2017

MAGAZINES

"Three Minutes to Midnight' editorial, Bulletin of the Atomic Scientists, January 1984.
Cluehaz, Toby, 'Peter Garrett: Relax With Max', *Roadrunner*, Volume 4, Nos 11 & 12, December 1981-January 1982

Coupe, Stuart, 'Rob Hirst on new material, Midnight Oil reunion', *Rolling Stone*, June 20, 2016
Creswell, Toby, 'Peter Garrett: A Journey of 1000 Miles Starts With One Step', *Rolling Stone*, 1985

Divola, Barry, 'Inside Midnight Oil's Game-Changing 10 to 1 Album', *Rolling Stone*, February 17, 2017

Fricke, David, 'Midnight Oil: Still Loud, Still Angry', *Rolling Stone*, October 25, 2017

Hall, Stan, 'Rob Hirst: Beats Are Burning', *Drumhead*, August, 2017

Leser, David, 'Peter and the Wolves', *Good Weekend*, August 15, 2009

McMillan, Andrew, 'Face the big light', *RAM*, November 9, 1984
McMillan, Andrew, 'Most Educated Punks in Oz. Midnight Oil', *RAM*, March 10, 1978
McMillan, Andrew, 'The Best of Both Worlds', *RAM*, February 13, 1985

Robertson, Donald, 'I'm a Performing Beast', *Roadrunner*, Volume 4, No 5, June 1981

Unknown, 'Midnight Oil: An integrity that bred loyalty', *Tell*, Volume 12, No4, November 1983-January 1984

White, Michael, 'Rob Hirst: Pursuing the Immaculate', *Rolling Stone*, 1985

Williams, Joy, 'Midnight Oil', *Artist Magazine*, July/August, 1984

Wolfe, Bill, 'Bubblin' Crude, *Spin*, August 1985

Wolfe, Bill, 'Up and Coming: Midnight Oil's Rob Hirst', publication unknown, October 1984

NEWSPAPERS

Baker, Christien, 'Timeline of the accident at Three Mile Island', *Patriot News*, March 22, 2009

Boehm, Mike, 'Finally, Midnight Oil Launches a Personal Tack, *LA Times*, October 2, 1993

Buckley, Amanda, 'NDP: No Dirty Politics?', *Sydney Morning Herald*, April 30, 1985

Coupe, Stuart, 'Midnight Oil – the work's paying off', *Sydney Morning Herald*, October 28, 1979

Dell'oso, Anna-Maria, 'The holocaust hits home', *Sydney Morning Herald*, April 11, 1984
Dent, Jackie, 'An American spy base hidden in Australia's outback', *New York Times*, November 23, 2017
Dorling, Philip, 'Pine Gap delivers US drone kills', *Sydney Morning Herald*, July 21, 2013

Fortescue, Elizabeth, 'Garrett makes PANDA his pet project', *Sydney Morning Herald*, May 24, 1985

Gibbs, Stephen, 'Jimmy Sharman, heir to the boxing tents, dies at 94', *Sydney Morning Herald*, April 26, 2006
Glover, Richard, 'Why Garrett chose politics over pop', *Sydney Morning Herald*, October 13, 1984

Hill, Robin, 'Garrett launches the NDP, the party of 'faith, hope and heart', *Sydney Morning Herald*, November 15, 1984
Holmes, Peter, 'Essential oils', *Sunday Age*, November 16, 1997
Humphries, Glen, 'A Midnight to Remember', *Illawarra Mercury*, December 3, 2016

Humphries, Glen, 'Garrett Is Back In Tune', *Illawarra Mercury*, July 23, 2016
Humphries, Glen, 'Oils: end of an era', Illawarra Mercury, June 5, 2003

Kruth, John, '15 years later Midnight Oil reunite to save us from oblivion', *The Observer*, August 5, 2017

Leser, David, 'Oils Still Burning', *Sydney Morning Herald*, November 11, 2017
Lewis, Daniel, 'Sharman the showman is an official bloody legend', *Sydney Morning Herald*, April 15, 2003

Noble, WS, 'A-bomb off: Double bang', *Melbourne Herald*, October 15, 1953

Parks, Alan, 'Midnight Oil founding member unveils songwriting secrets, *Northern Star*, August 13, 2014
Pierce, John, 'Cutbacks deal Tasmania new economic blows', *Sydney Morning Herald*, August 7, 1982

St John, Ed, 'Oils on the water help a troubled JJJ', *Sydney Morning Herald*, January 19, 1985
Strauss, Duncan, 'The Midnight Oil Bubbles Up From Down Under', *LA Times*, August 7, 1985
Sutherland, Donnie, 'Sunday Extra – Sounds', *Sydney

Morning Herald, October 21, 1984

Testro, Ron, 'A blonde bombshell blew up Maralinga', *Melbourne Argus*, June 20, 1956
Thomson, Robert, 'No clear winner but a disarmament victory', *Sydney Morning Herald*, December 3, 1984
Thomson, Robert, and Steketee, Mike, 'NDP alters stand as PM attacks', *Sydney Morning Herald*, November 21, 1984
Totaro, Paola, 'Garrett plans new anti-nuclear party', *Sydney Morning Herald*, May 2, 1985

Unknown, 'ACTU calls for halt to atomic tests', *Sydney Tribune*, August 7, 1957
Unknown, 'Atomic blast ends wait at Maralinga', *Canberra Times*, September 28, 1956
Unknown, 'Atomic explosion at Emu Field: Another soon', *Wagga Daily Advertiser*, October 16, 1953
Unknown, 'Commons hears about Australian Aborigines', *Canberra Times*, February 2, 1957
Unknown, 'Garrett's Senate try fails: Mason In', *Canberra Times*, January 9, 1985
Unknown, 'Garrett to burn midnight oil if elected', *Canberra Times*, December 2, 1984
Unknown, 'It's Mason for the Senate', *Sydney Morning*

Herald, January 9, 1985

Unknown, 'Midnight Oil's Senate candidate', *Sydney Morning Herald*, October 8, 1984

Unknown, 'No escape for captive balloons, says Beale', *Canberra Times*, August 15, 1957

Unknown, 'Radioactive dogs', *Beverley Times*, January 31, 1957

Unknown, 'Renison plunges to a $6.5 million loss', *Sydney Morning Herald*, August 27, 1982

Unknown, 'Shutdowns for Mt Lyell', *Sydney Morning Herald*, August 7, 1982

Zuel, Bernard, 'Midnight Memories', *Sydney Morning Herald*, November 1, 2012

WEBSITES

'Andrew James – an autobiography', Andrew James, heartburstmusic.com

'Backgrounder on the Three Mile Island Accident', United States Nuclear Regulatory Commission, accessed February 15, 2018

Bell, Steve, 'A look back at Midnight Oil's landmark LP *Red Sails in the Sunset*', Themusic.com.au, October 2, 2014

Benedict, Kennette, 'Doomsday clockwork', The Bulletin of the Atomic Scientists', thebulletin.org
Blackwood, Gemma, 'Australia Day: A Survivor's Film Guide', The Conversation, January 26, 2016

Gallagher, Ryan, 'The US spy hub in the heart of Australia', The Intercept, August 20, 2017
Gifford, Peter, 'Ask Giffo!', Powderworkers, Facebook page, April 30, 2017

Hirst, Rob, 'Imaginary Noise opening night speech', artisan.org.au, September 13, 2013

Lamb, Robert, 'How a Nuclear Meltdown Works', howstuffworks.com
Launay, Nick, 'Midnight Oil's Rob Hirst Takes Us Track by Track Through *Flat Chat*, www.launay.com

McCarthy, Sean, 'Power and the Passion: An Interview with Midnight Oil', Pop Matters, May 6, 2013
Morelli, Laura, 'A round or two for a pound or two: The touring tent boxing circuses', sbs.com.au, June 4, 2017

Patsy, Edina, 'Midnight Oil Peter Garrett Interview', Noise11.com, May 5, 2016

Swales, Kris, 'Midnight Oil: Power and the Passion', TheMusic.com.au, September 26, 2013

Thomas, Bryan, 'Power and the Passion: Midnight Oil's Aggro Agit-Pop and the '80s Australian Invasion', Nightflight, May 1, 2017

Tynan, Liz, 'Dig for secrets: the lessons of Maralinga's Vixen B Trials', The Conversation, July 26, 2013

Tynan, Liz, 'Sixty years on, the Maralinga bomb tests remind us not to put security over safety', The Conversation, September 26, 2016

PODCASTS/ONLINE INTERVIEWS

Foulds, Darren, and Harbron, Robin, *Comfortable Place on the Couch* podcast, 2017

Interview with Jim Moginie, *Depth Perception* podcast, Episode Eight, Season Two, www.dppod.com, December 20, 2014

Reding, Mal, interview with Peter Garrett, Mal Reding Interview Archive, recorded 1984 malreding.com

MOVIES and DVDS

Midnight Oil, *40,000 Watt RSL*, Sony, 2017
Midnight Oil: 1984, directed by Ray Argall, Madman Entertainment, 2018
Midnight Oil: *Best of Both Worlds*, Midnight Oil Enterprises/ABC, 2004
Midnight Oil, *MTV Unplugged*, Sony Music, 2017
Midnight Oil, *Only The Strong: The Making of 10,9,8,7,6,5,4,3,2,1*, Sony Music, 2017
Midnight Oil, *Ellis Park: The Concert*, Sony Music, 2017
Midnight Oil, *Moments in Space*, Sony Music, 2017
One Night Stand, directed by John Duigan, Hoyts Distribution, 1984
Reach for the Sky, directed by Lewis Gilbert, Rank Organisation, 1956

CDs

Midnight Oil, *10,9,8,7,6,5,4,3,2,1*, CBS Records, 1982
Midnight Oil, *Red Sails In the Sunset*, CBS, 1984
Midnight Oil, *Scream In Blue*, Columbia, 1992
Midnight Oil, *Flat Chat*, SonyBMG, 2006
Midnight Oil, *Essential Oils*, Sony, 2012
Midnight Oil, *Lasseter's Gold*, Sony Music, 2017
Sennett, Sean, *Full Tank* liner notes, Sony/ATV

Music, 2017

Stafford, Andrew, *Overflow Tank* liner notes, Sony/ATV Music, 2017

If you liked this book why not check out my others, all which are available through my micropublishing company Last Day of School? Go on … I'll be your best friend.
(www.lastdayofschool.net)

The Slab
24 Stories of Beer in Australia

Beer. You know it and, chances are, you love it. But you might not know the part beer has played in Australian history. Right from the start beer was there. It was on board The Endeavour when Captain Cook set sail for Australia. It was drunk not long after the First Fleet landed in Botany Bay.

It was there when World War I soldiers got a skinful and ran riot in the streets of Sydney. It was there during the era of six o'clock closing where people were still drinking it long after the little hand had passed the six. It was even there when it really shouldn't have been - when Canberra declared itself an alcohol-free zone.

What? You didn't know the nation's capital used to be dry? Well, then you need this book. You'll also find out just what the hell Voltron has to do with Victoria Bitter.

"History as it should be written. With beer. About beer. Crisp. Refreshing. Won't cause bloat."
John Birmingham, author of Leviathan

"I thought I'd been asked to review Christos Tsiolkas' The Slap and was pleasantly surprised to find myself reading about beer. The Slab is a full-bodied book, with a fruity aftertaste and a nose that carries the slightest hint of sawdust and vomit. I suggest you XXXX it."
David Hunt, author of Girt

James Squire: The Biography

After getting caught swiping a few chickens from a neighbour, James Squire was sentenced to seven years in Sydney Cove. You could say it was the best thing he ever did – it led to him become a brewer, policeman, property tycoon, respected citizen and a bloody rich guy.

All because of the theft of a few chooks.

But if all you know about James Squire is what you've read on labels on beer bottles, then you really don't know that much at all. This book – the first biography of Squire – separates the facts from the well-known myths about his life. He never stowed away on the First Fleet ship carrying female convicts, didn't get lashed for stealing the ingredients to make beer and might not have been the first person to grow hops in Australia.

He was also a man who may have used a false name on his daughter's birth certificate, loathed people who cut down trees on his property and got along far better with the natives than most of the other white newcomers.

Along the way you'll also discover a few other things about Sydney Cove, including Captain Arthur Phillip's efforts to get his hands on some Aboriginal heads for a friend, early Australians' fondness for cider rather than beer, the fight rival brewer John Boston had over a dead pig and the marine who tried to trade his hat for an Aboriginal child.

Friday Night at the Oxford

The story that led to reunion of legendary band Tumbleweed. An in-depth look at Sunday Painters, a band decades ahead of their time. Iconic shows like HOPE, HyFest and the Steel City Sound exhibition. These are just of the more than 100 stories about Wollongong bands and events written by journalist Glen Humphries for the *Illawarra Mercury*, from 1997 through to 2018, and his own shortlived website Dragster.

The 200-plus pages of *Friday Night at the Oxford* provide a snapshot of what happened in the Wollongong music scene over the last 20-odd years – the bands, the venues, the events. It's a celebration of the music of a city.

So dig it.

EBOOKS

The Six-Pack
Stories from the World of Beer

From stories of monks making beer, to rumours of an unpleasant secret "ingredient" in a world-famous drink, there are plenty of great stories about beer. And six of them are captured in this ebook.

Beer is Fun!

Oh look, it's the best moments from Beer is Your Friend, the blog that won a national beer writing award and also inspired Dale to leave a comment "give ur self an uppercut u oxygen thief".

Clearly Dale wasn't on the judging panel. Which is a good thing too, otherwise I wouldn't have won that trophy – and who doesn't like winning trophies? Why should you buy this book? Because it's 300-plus and it'll cost you just $2. What else in life will give you loads of entertainment for just $2? Go on, buy it. If you don't like it, I'll give you your money back. Well, that's a lie, I won't give you a cent, because I plan on holidaying in The Bahamas with the $2 you give me.

www.ingramcontent.com/pod-product-compliance
Lightning Source LLC
Chambersburg PA
CBHW071906290426
44110CB00013B/1300